Heaven to Earth

Inspirations from God

Freda Westnedge

ISBN 978-1-64416-896-7 (paperback)
ISBN 978-1-64416-898-1 (hardcover)
ISBN 978-1-64416-897-4 (digital)

Christian Faith Publishing, Inc.
832 Park Avenue
Meadville, PA 16335
www.christianfaithpublishing.com

Printed in the United States of America

To our loving wife and mother, Freda Westnedge, who spent her life showing us what a true "Christ follower" looks like.
We love and miss you!

Contents

From the Family...13

Foreword...15

A Word from the Author..16

A Birthday Wish 19

A Choice 20

A Day at Play 23

A Gift..26

A Glimpse 28

A Heart's Thought..31

A Heavy Load 32

A Hug from Jesus 35

A Letter to a Friend 36

A Letter to God..39

A Message 40

A Moment of Beauty...42

A Mother's Prayer..43

A Need to Pray...45

A New Burden 46

A Painful Heart 48

A Prayer 51

A Prayer for Steve..52

A Seeking Heart 54

A Thought to Remember 55

A True Heart 56

All Glory to You, Lord...58

All Life's Treasures 59

Almost 62

An Outreached Hand...63

Another Love Letter 64

Back Home 66

Blessings..67

Blood Red 69

Bringing Hope 70
Burdens for the Lost..72
Can I Ask Why? 74
Carry Me...75
Children's Choir...76
Christmas Prayer for You..77
Come, Lord..79
Daddy, Did You See Me?..80
Drenched in Love...82
Don't Wait...83
Dry Those Tears 84
Encouraging Retreat...85
Experience Through Pain 86
Extraordinary Grace 88
Far Away Friends...89
Father of Heaven 91
Finding Our Home 92
Food for My Soul...95
Forever Close..96
Forever Loving 98
Forever Reaching..100
Friendship..101
Friendship Wings...102
Garment of Praise...103
Gifts from the Heart..104
Give It to Jesus 106
Giving..107
Go Sweet Spirit 108
God is Near..111
God's Blessings 112
Grace Carried Me...114
Grandmother 116
Guard My Tongue...117
Guide Me...119
Happy Birthday, Daddy, How's Heaven Today?..................120
Happy Birthday, Friend...122

Hard Trials 123
He Comforts Me..124
He Gave 125
He Hears My Heart..127
He is Light 128
He Loves Me 130
He Understands 131
He Waits for Me..132
Healing Love...134
Healing through Forgiveness 136
Heart of a Friend...138
Heartache of Rejection 139
Heaven's Growing Sweeter.................................140
Heavenly Angels..141
Heavenly Messengers...144
He'll be There 145
His Beauty 146
His Grace 147
His Presence 148
His Presence in the Night...................................149
His Word 150
Home Away from Home.....................................152
Home Front 153
I Saw a Life Slip Away Today.............................154
I See 156
I Shall Not Want...157
If I Could..158
If Only They Knew 159
If You Should Remember 162
I'll Be Away for a While.....................................164
I'm Hurting...165
In His Arms 166
In His Presence..169
In Search of Love...170
Inner Healing 173
It's Only the Beginning 174

It's True! I'm Forgiven!...176

Jesus Cares!...178

Jesus Loves Me! 179

Just Say Thank You 180

Keeping My Eyes on You...181

Ladies Camp Retreat 182

Led to Fast 184

Let My Voice Ring Loud 186

Let Us Love You 189

Letter to a Lonely Heart 190

Lifeline...192

Longing for Jesus...193

Looking Ahead...195

Lost at Sea 196

Love Gently Blooms...198

Love Letter to God...200

Love Never Fades 203

Love Ran Deep...204

Love? What Does it Really Mean? 206

Lover of My Soul...209

Make Me a Blessing...210

Mary Did Your Heart Break?...213

Memory Book...214

Merry Christmas, Daddy...216

Morning Hideaway 218

Mother...219

Mother's Day...220

Moving Away 221

My Best Friend...223

My Brother, My Friend 224

My Cyber Friend...227

My Dad...228

My Dad Is Home 231

My Love for You...232

My Love Is Still Here...235

My Mother, My Friend 238

My Spirit Soars..240
No Number Needed..243
No One Can Know..244
No Record in Heaven...246
Nursery..247
O Death Where Is Thy Sting................................248
One Day...250
Only a Moment...252
Only One Love..254
Only You...255
Open the Door..256
Pain So Deep..257
Plow Up My Field, Lord!....................................258
Power of the Spirit...260
Praise Him!..262
Prayer of Love..263
Prayer Partners...265
Prayers Of the Saints..266
Purity...268
Putting Away the Doubts....................................270
Putting On Christ...271
Reaching Out..272
Reflections of Love...273
Rejoice!...276
Remembering the '50s..278
Remember the Call...280
Reporting for Orders...282
Rest for the Spirit..283
Retreat of a Lonely Heart...................................284
Riches Untold...288
Safe in the Lighthouse.......................................290
Seasons of Pain...291
She Is Not Forgotten...292
She Ran the Race...294
She's Running in Heavenly Meadows.......................295
Shine Forth His Light..296

Someone Is Praying 298
Someone's Hurting 299
Spiritual Fight 300
Spring of Hope 302
Stay on Course 304
Story Time 306
Strayed from the Path 308
Strength Through Adversity 309
Teacher 311
Tears of War 312
Tears Through the Storm 314
Tenfold 316
Thank You 317
Thankful for the Little Things 318
The Angels Rejoice 319
The Bible 320
The Body of Christ 323
The Bond of Friendships 326
The Bride 328
The Day We Embrace 330
The Fall 331
The Feast 334
The Gift of a Prayer 337
The Gift of Easter 338
The Goal 340
The Last Words 342
The Operation 344
The Race 345
The Remembrance Book—Malachi 3:16 346
The Rock 348
The Search 350
The Struggle 351
The True Cry 353
The Work Starts Here 354
They Sang to Me 356
This Moment and Forever 357

This World Cannot Hold..358
Thoughts from the Heart..360
Thoughts of the Heart...361
Touch of the Spirit...362
Troubled Soul...363
True Love..364
View From the Ferry...365
Wait No More...366
Walking in the Trials..368
Warmth of His Presence..370
Water My Soul..372
We Can Overcome..373
Wedding Day...375
When It's Time..376
When Life Begins...378
When, Lord?..380
When Words Are Not Enough..382
When You Think of Me...385
Where Is My Place, Lord?...386
Without the Anointing...388
Witnessing on the Highway...389
Words..390
Worldly Pleasures..391
You Are My Hiding Place..393
You Love Me Just as I Am...394
Your Love..396

Writings, Stories, and Love Letters to God........................397

A Rose, A Heart...399
A Rose in Bloom..400
Eternal Healing...401
For the Love of My Dad..402
Forever Place..404
From the Lord...405
Goldie Finds a Home...406

I'm Not There Yet...408
In Search of a Friend 410
Lord I'm Waiting...412
Love Covers It All..413
The Family...414
Mary Jane and the Bear Jamboree.............................416
My Friend Jack...418
My Heart Cries 422
My Life I Give...423
My Love, My Devotion, My Heart..............................424
Spreading Your Wings 426
Tell Me..427
The Long Search 428
The Thief of Busyness 430
Touching God's Heart...432
Watch and Pray..433
What Is a Mother?...434
Wisdom to Change 436
Wounded Soul 437
Dedication Poem...438

From the Family

We would like to give you some insight into our loving wife and mother, Freda Westnedge.

Freda was born in Cramerton, North Carolina, in May 1946. She married the love of her life, David, in June 1964. They shared fifty-two wonderful years together and had three amazing daughters.

Freda came to know Jesus as her Lord and Savior in 1977 when her brother Danny led her to Christ. From the day she asked Jesus into her heart, she became a vessel of love on this earth. An earlier experience with Jesus as a child at eight years old had prepared her heart for this day, and she lovingly gave her whole life to serving God.

She was the most loving, giving, caring, and humble person we have ever known. She loved everyone, and she loved unconditionally.

She listened and faithfully obeyed the Lord whenever he spoke to her, no matter what He asked her to do. She began writing poetry shortly after making Jesus her Lord, and she always shared with us the words that God had given to her.

Her desire was to someday put the Lord's words in a book. She was called home to be with Jesus before her someday ever arrived. As a family, we are blessed to share her writings with you. We have included everything that she wrote; mostly poems, but also some songs, stories, writings, and "love letters to God" are in here. We have dated those that she put a date on, but many of them were handwritten, or they were on old typing paper! Her writings spanned from the late '70s to the time of her death.

We hope you enjoy them all!

In loving memory of Freda Westnedge
May 1946–February 2017

Foreword[*]

As I sit here in my dining room, my mind drifts back to the first time the Lord spoke to my heart about writing this book. I thought to myself, Lord, what could I possibly have to offer the world that would be of any importance? The answer to my question was very plain: "You have Me Freda, and I'm what the world needs."

That's right, I thought, I have Jesus living in my heart, and He is the most important person in my life. Mark 12:30 sums it up perfectly, "Thou shalt love thy God with all thy heart, and with all thy soul, and with all thy mind, and with all thy strength."

I want to express in the following pages my love for God through my writings and poems. I want to relate through my simplicity how I visualize the hand of God on my life over these past years.

My prayer for you, the reader, is that I in no way want this book to take away from your daily reading of God's word, which is our strength and our lifeline.

---

[*] Written by Freda. She was already in the first stages of preparing to write her book.

A Word from the Author

My story's not a gory one
I've never been on drugs
I have not lived a dirt-filled life
You'd sweep beneath the rugs
I've written of things I lived through
When I was but a child
Some are really very neat
Others not so mild
I will not come to you with words
Too big to understand
The poems I write are simple ones
Given me by the Master's hand
If you should come and ask of me
A poem expressing love
You can be sure that I would pray
And seek my Father above
He is my only source for words
They come from within my heart
I write of things I feel and see
Expressing "light" and not the dark
I always ask of Him to be
A vessel for his use
I know that if my heart's sincere
My God will not refuse
He is so much a part of me
My every breath I take
I want the words He speaks through me
To be heard for His name's sake
I want the world to know the Lord
As their dear and special friend
I want them to accept His blood
He shed for all their sin

They should be told how much He cares
And wants to meet their needs
If they will have repented hearts
And fall upon their knees
God wants the world to know His love
So let's reach out a hand
And let the spirit flow from us
All over this wonderful land.

A Birthday Wish

If I could have but just one wish
This is what I'd say
"Dear God, please keep her in your care
Throughout her special day."
I would pray that He would give
You joy and happiness
To help you be so bold and strong
To live victorious
I would pray for Him to place
His angels from above
That they might sing you heavenly songs
And to say to you "You're loved."

A Choice

My heart was broken, as I listened to you talk …
   I heard the tears in your voice …
Oh, how I prayed for strength from above—
   My friend, please make the right choice …

I wish your pain, I could take away …
   That power is not mine to do …
Your heavenly Father, and Him alone—
   Will take this pain from you …

I know it's hard to see right now …
   This too, shall come to pass …
The heartache you're feeling this very moment—
   Though it hurts, it will not last …

The important thing to always remember—
   To love the Lord with all of your heart …
He will guide and direct your path—
   Let Him give you a brand-new start …

There's no greater joy than to follow God's will—
   Just pray—He will reveal …
As we give up our plans, to seek after His—
   Our lives He will fulfill …

For things unseen by your eyes today,
   could be what He has in mind …
Your burdens, dreams, and fears—
   Will be handled in His perfect time …

Faith is the substance of things hoped for ...
    Like a child, you must now believe ...
That your Father in heaven knows your heart—
    He will answer your every plea ...

Just keep your heart open to Him my friend ...
    Listen for that small still voice ...
He's speaking now—can you hear Him, dear one?
    He'll help you to make the right choice ...

Written July 9, 2002

A Day at Play

Our mom went through a stage where she collected and sold dolls. She loved them so much! She would even take them to the mall in a stroller; it was so cute! She loved to talk to people as they looked into her stroller and realized it was a doll, not a baby! Many times, she would tell them about Jesus! She just LOVED people!

This is a poem she wrote about her dollies.

At first I thought I was dreaming,
    I woke up with a start …
Jumped out of bed, ran downstairs,
    And there was *Young at Heart* …

She had the babies on the couch,
    Some were in the chair …
I heard her yell to *Party Girl*,
    "Let's boogie—let down your hair!" …

Come on, babies, get out of bed …
    Now's the time to play …
Mom's asleep up in her room,
    So I'm in charge today …

The babies got together,
    To decide just what to do …
Leaping Lambs was hungry,
    So they made a pot of stew …

Best Friend Bear, she made a cake …
    Put candy on the top …
When the babies saw her work,
    The dancing would not stop …

When they finished up the food,
    It was time to hit the road …
The RV now was ready,
    They began to pack and load …

The twins had been so busy,
    With plans that they had made …
They knew that all the babies,
    Would love the new arcade …

When they went inside, they saw,
    The Easter bunny there …
They ran up to him, pulling his leg—
    Playing with his ears and hair …

He gave them all a candy egg,
    Saying, "Kids, you need to go …
Your mommie called me on the phone,
    You worried her, you know!

So off they went to hurry home,
    For now it had turned cold …
They were laughing and cracking up,
    From the stories *Precious* told …

Their mommie saw them coming,
    She ran into the street …
She threw her arms around them tight,
    As she began to weep …

They were happy to be home,
   Their day now, was complete ...
Mommie whispered in their ears,
   "Sleep, my children, sleep" ...

A Gift

God is love—
    We are His hands…
You can make a difference—
    It's all in His plans…

We each have been made—
    In His image you see …
We're here for a purpose—
    Both you and me …

Some have talents,
    That reach far and wide …
Over the seas—
    Or Montana's big sky …

It doesn't matter if you're rich,
    Or if you're poor …
What matter's—are you ready?
    When God opens a door?

Maybe your gift,
    Is praying for the lost?
Maybe its missions,
    As you count the cost …

The cost being your life,
    Given to others …
Ready to minister—
    To your sisters and brothers …

Maybe your gift,
  Is working with your hands ...
Letting God use you—
  Wherever He can ...

Maybe your hands,
  Will build churches or schools ...
For worship and learning—
  He'll supply all your tools ...

Is cooking for the hungry,
  A gift you will be giving?
Offering hope—
  And shelter for their living?

Maybe you're a mother?
  Such a gift to behold ...
A precious little life—
  Through your hands will unfold ...

Tenderly, gently,
  As you guide them each day ...
God gives you wisdom—
  He's the truth—He's the way ...

Witten July 11, 2002

A Glimpse

I prayed for you today,
   I shed many tears.
The Father's love
   was so very near.

He wants you to know
   that He loves you so,
and He has carried
   your heavy load.

He gave me a glimpse
   of your faithfulness;
I saw how you've walked with Him
   through much distress.

I saw His arms
   around you tight,
I saw Him holding you
   all through the night.

I saw Him wiping
   each and every tear,
it must have been
   through many a year;

For it seemed so long
   that He held you there,
all snuggled up
   in a "great big chair."

He was stroking your hair
   Saying, "Hush now, child,
your Father's here,
   let's talk for a while."

You poured your heart
   into His ear,
you told Him everything—
   You had no fear.

You felt so warm
   all aglow inside,
as the two of you sat
   and He held you tight.

He gave you peace
   through your questions there,
as He so gently
   kept stroking your hair.

You looked at Him
   and then you smiled,
you knew you'd been there
   for quite a while.

You didn't want
   to leave His chair,
you wanted to stay
   all snuggled there.

He said to you
   "Come tomorrow, child,
we'll sit again
   and talk awhile."

I thank Him for
    this glimpse of you,
and the gift of carrying
    your burden too.

So don't let this world
    now get you down,
Your prayers are being heard
    in the "Heavenly Realm" …

A Heart's Thought

My Lord, my Shepherd, and my King
You mean the world to me
My rock, my refuge, and my strength
The One from Galilee
I feel the warmth within Your love
Your arms around me close
Of all the loves within this world
I love You, Lord, the most
No other One could meet my need
No one could satisfy
Or fill this longing in my soul
To be close by Your side
I'm waiting, Lord, for You to come
And take away your Bride
A glorious morning that will be
When rapture fills the sky
To live with You eternally
Lord, that's my heart's desire
Prepare me now to come to You
And help me not to tire
Reach out Your hand through me, my Lord
To others that I meet
And with the love that flows from You
I'll lay them at Your feet.
And with the love that flows from You,
I'll lay them at Your feet

Originally written by Freda as a song

A Heavy Load

Just sitting here thinking of you today,
wondering just how you are.
I wish we could live closer;
I wish it weren't so far.

I miss the times we had, my friend,
the special things we shared;
I miss the smile upon your face,
the special way you cared.

I miss the talks we used to have,
till early morning hour;
We always seemed to end our time,
praying in Jesus' power.

I miss the walks we had together,
down that old dirt road;
The time so quickly passed back then,
as we shared our *heavy load*.

I could tell you anything,
that was upon my heart;
Knowing it would stay with you,
and never would depart.

So many problems we could solve,
walking the old dirt road;
I wonder where you are today,
are you carrying a *heavy load*?

If you are, remember, friend,
Jesus has walked that road;
So look up to the one today,
who promises to carry our load ...

A Hug from Jesus

I opened the door so gently.
   There in front I see ...
A beautiful floral arrangement.
   I was told it was for me ...

Carefully I opened the card attached ...
   I felt the love that flowed.
Sent to me by a precious friend,
   I've come to love and know ...

Although her name was written there,
   The gift was from above.
My friend was touched by the Master's hand,
   To send me a "Special Hug" ...

All wrapped in beauty, God's great design.
   The fragrance filled the air.
Roses so delicate, carnations of pink,
   Filling my eyes everywhere ...

Spatters of colors all intertwined,
   To fill my heart with joy ...
I felt so warm and loved today,
   Like a child with a brand-new toy ...

To you, my friend I say "Thank you" ...
   To Jesus, "I love You So" ...
You've touched my heart so deeply ...
   More than you'll ever know ...

Written June 25, 2004

A Letter to a Friend

You sure have meant a lot to me,
    throughout my Christian walk.
Although I've had some bad times,
    you've helped me through our talks.

The wisdom God has given you,
    I know can never be bought.
It's come from many painful nights,
    because His face you've sought.

I know you've had some hard times,
    I've seen God bring you through.
Because your trust in Him was great,
    my faith it has renewed.

Spiritual gifts we should strive for,
    that's what the Bible says.
If I could have just one for me,
    I'd take the gift of kindness.

That's what I've seen from both of you,
    throughout the years gone past.
If I could take a lesson from you,
    I know my gift would last.

The love you show to everyone,
    is overwhelming to me.
I know it's God working through you,
    because you give it so free.

The many lives that you have touched,
    I could never number.
Because you have travailed in prayer,
    and never have you slumbered.

You've ran the race and fought it well,
    you're headed down the homestretch.
Don't let your faith be wavered now,
    just hold on to your catch.

You're venturing out in fields untold.
    what will they hold for you?
I know whatever lies ahead,
    our God will see you through.

So I must now tell you goodbye;
    but not for long I know.
Cause I'll see you in the eastern skies,
    if not on this earth below.

A Letter to God

Dear God
How much longer shall it be?
Their eyes are so blinded
To the good things of Thee
Their security is in silver and gold
And in "things"
If only they would trust
In the goodness of knowing Thee
They let fears overcome them
Till they're tossed in despair
Yet they will not see You
Lingering there
If only they could see
Your love and Your strength
They would come to that calmness
You give from within
This peace
This love
This strength
That You give
Dear God, would You please
Give it to my friends!

Inspired by the Holy Spirit,
As given to Freda Westnedge

A Message

Rejoice, my son,
   for I am with thee;
The grief you now bear,
   is for necessity.

You hurt inside,
   for your loved one whose gone;
I understand child,
   and will help you be strong.

Release it, my son,
   for the tears they must flow;
I will give you my strength,
   and for your face; a new glow.

Lift up your head,
   hold it high;
You'll have your reunion,
   when I come in the sky.

When the dead in Christ,
   shall rise in the air;
You'll all live together,
   and reign with me there.

But now my son,
   I have work for you;
Be strong and help others,
   with grief to work through.

Know I'm your God,
    that I'm watching you too;
For I speak in my name,
    YOUR STRENGTH IS RENEWED!

Received February 23, 1983

A Moment of Beauty

Powder white clouds
forming beauty in the sky.
Birds all abreast
with a wondering eye;

Seeking their food
from the green grass below.
Sipping on raindrops
not a care do they know.

A soft wind is blowing
as it ushers in spring.
Children now playing
in the park on a swing.

Fields full of flowers
like spatters of ink;
Dazzling orange, bright yellow
some pink.

God's great creation
all are at play.
This moment of beauty,
my reward for today.

A Mother's Prayer

My beautiful precious daughter
   oh Lord, You've been so good
To give to me my heart's desire
   help me raise her the way I should
Give me strength, Lord, day by day
   through the good times and the bad
Give me patience, love, and kindness
   to help her when she's sad
Give to me Your Wisdom
   that I might guide her through
The youthful years ahead of her
   and teach her Your word is true
I want a special attitude
   to praise and worship You
Though bad times may beset her
   she'll know You will see her through
I need the strength only You can give
   for the burdens I must bear
While teaching her the right from wrong
   still letting her know I care
And for the times of tears, Lord
   I know they lie ahead
Give me Holy Boldness
   to speak the words You've said
So when the world shall beckon her
   help me pull back the strings
And teach her that our happiness
   lies in Your water springs
Help me relate the joys we have
   in service unto You
That through obedience to Your word
   she'll know Your love is true

A Need to Pray[*]

As I sit here and ponder
Over things throughout my day
I feel my Lord is teaching me
Of a special need to pray
The one who crossed my path today
Caused a twinge of pain
To see his sad and lonely face
My cheerfulness was in vain
I hurt within my heart for him
As he turned to go his way
I wanted to run and say to him
"Let Jesus help you today."
I know my Lord is teaching me
The world I cannot save
But I can take a bended knee
"Dear God, heal him today!"

January 5, 1983

---

[*] Titled by family

A New Burden

Dear Father in heaven,
    hallowed be Thy name.
I have a special prayer, my Lord—
    it's not a rhyme or a game.

I've been a little lax dear God,
    in praying for the lost.
I have not thought about your pain—
    your agony or cost.

I want to be your vessel, Lord,
    but I get so very weak;
I let my eyes slip off of you,
    and your will I do not seek.

I need a fresh awakening, Lord,
    "A New Burden" in my heart.
If You will grant this wish to me,
    I'll make a brand-new start.

I'll go right out into my world,
proclaiming that You save—
Teaching those you bring to me,
You are the truth, the life, the way.

The little lady in her house,
    just sitting all alone—
I'll tell her that You reign on high,
    beside the Father's throne.

And all the children on the streets,
    I'll tell them of your love—
And how they can find happiness,
    and live with You above.

The ones who lie so sick in bed,
    I'll tell them that you heal—
And if they'll pray and seek your face,
    You'll be to them so real.

I'll even tell the prisoners
    down in the lonely jails;
That you can give them freedom—
    without one cent for bail.

I'll be so very careful,
    to greet my neighbor, Lord—
To pray for love and wisdom,
    and wait for an open door.

Is there one today, my Lord,
    that I may go and touch?
If so, Father, direct my path,
    and I'll thank You very much …

A Painful Heart

Lord, if I had a dollar for every time I thought of You,
I would be a millionaire by now.
When I awake, my thoughts turn toward You.
Many times there is sadness in my heart.
I pray You can understand,
the deepest cries from the depth of my soul.
Even though my words are not spoken,
I pray You feel my hearts pain.
Within me, I know You do.
The pain is so intense,
my heart feels like it will burst at any moment.
Is this the pain You felt, Lord,
when you prayed in the garden?
Were You crying over the sin,
You saw in my life even then?
My tears run like rain,
falling down a window pane.
When I think of how I've hurt You, Lord,
I die a thousand deaths inside,
for the pain I've caused You.
Not to mention the pain I've caused myself.
I weep in silence.
In the stillness of the night.
My sin is ever before me.
Alone I must bare this burden,
as not to inflict pain on those I love.
Lord, I pray they never know how I've let You down.
Your love means more to me than life itself.
I stand in awe at your mercy, oh God, my Father.
So undeserving am I of your kindness to me.
Will I ever be free from this pain within?
They say time heals all wounds.

The hands are slowly passing by.
Each moment seems like eternity ... eternity!
A time I used to look forward to;
A time now that echo's pain within my heart.
When I will have to stand before You.
Looking into your eyes of love.
Knowing the price You paid for me.
Knowing my sins hung You on the Tree ...

A Prayer

Wipe my tears, Lord,
   with Thy precious love.
Send Your peace,
   from heaven above.

Ease this pain, Lord,
   within my heart.
Help me to know,
   You'll never depart.

Walk close beside me,
   everyday.
Take all my fears,
   and drive them away.

Teach me Your word,
   help me be strong.
Let me praise You,
   in a heavenly song.

Send Your spirit,
   deep into my soul.
Filled with power,
   that I may be bold.

Guide me by,
   Your mighty hand.
To spread Your word,
   throughout this land …

A Prayer for Steve

Hello, Lord, it's me, your daughter—
Standing here needing your touch …
There's no one else I trust with my heart …
Lord, I love you so much …

Sometimes I have a hard time, Lord,
understanding why you're always there …
How wonderful it is to feel this assurance,
knowing you always care …

Hello, Lord, can you come a little closer,
I need you to hear this one …
Steve is lying very ill,
his life is next to done …

I need your ministering angels,
all around his room …
Surround him with your *Heavenly Choir*—
he may be coming soon …

I need you, Lord, to comfort him—
give him Your peace within …
Tell him, Lord, how much you love him,
as the angels usher him in …

Only you, Lord, know the hour,
when we are called to meet with you …
You could heal him in an instant,
You have that power too …

I'm here on his behalf, Lord,
asking for your perfect will ...
Life and death are in your hands, Lord,
yet I will praise you still ...

He's fought so hard, Lord,
in days gone by ...
He's weak and tired—
the family is nigh ...

You alone have loved him,
far greater than anyone ...
So if the time is now, Lord,
please let your angels come ...

Written March 31, 2001

A Seeking Heart

I'm not ashamed of You, my Lord,
I'll hold my head up high.
Without You in my life, dear God,
this child would surely die.
You've brought me from the pit of despair,
You gave new life to me.
You placed a love within my heart,
a love that comes only from Thee ...
You've taught me to walk by faith, dear Lord,
no worry in the problems I see.
You've been so faithful throughout the years,
my Praise goes only to Thee ...
I shudder to think where I might be,
had You not spared my life.
As I called out Your Name on high,
seeking *Truth*, *Wisdom*, and *Light*.
As mountains spring forth,
as rivers flow,
as sunshine brings warmth,
to Your children below ...
I'll forever remember,
that cold dreary night,
when You my Jesus, filled me with *Love*—
filled me with life ...

Written May 21, 2005

A Thought to Remember

As you start this busy day,
have you kneeled before the Lord to pray?

Have you thanked Him for His love,
have you thanked the God above?

Do you praise Him in every way,
for the miracles he gives each day?

Do you see there is no cost,
because for you, His Son He lost?

Do you thank Him every morn,
for the fact that you're reborn!?

Do you praise Him for the sky,
and its beauty money can't buy?

Do you thank Him for your health,
all your treasures, and your wealth?

Do you praise Him for ones so near,
who give their love all through the year?

Have you thanked Him for His love,
have you thanked the God above?

A True Heart

The Spirit of Depression—
   the enemy of my soul;
It preys upon me,
   leaving me so cold.

No warning it gives,
   springing from within—
Paralyzing my thoughts,
   keeping me from Him.

The walls seem so high
   as I try reaching Him in prayer;
Too anguished even for tears,
   in the Spirit I know He's there.

Deliver me speedily
   from this affliction, Father,
For my spirit is truly
   overwhelmed within me.

The tears now flow
   out of control.
Come heal my broken heart,
   bind the wounds of this hurting soul.

Speak once again,
   Your forgiveness I need;
Take away my selfish heart,
   oh! Father, I plead.

Give me a humble heart
tender and true—
With one goal in mind,
TO LOVE ONLY YOU!

All Glory to You, Lord

I bring You all the *Glory*,
  Lord, it all belongs to You …
I want your love, through me, dear Lord,
  to come shining through …

I want to be your hands and feet,
  walking through the city streets—
Guiding others to the cross,
  sharing how You paid the cost.

Open up my eyes to see,
  brokenhearted ones in need.
Wounded soldiers for the cross,
  striving to bring in the lost …

The fields are white for harvest,
  we know you're coming soon.
Although we know no hour,
  it could be night or noon …

The pearly gates will open,
  the book of life shall be read …
Names of saints gone before us,
  will be called like Jesus said …

All crowns and jewels will be given,
  each one will have their reward …
One by one we will step up—
  and place them at the feet of our Lord …

All Life's Treasures

I had all life's *Treasures*
of the world we know here.
Family, friends,
loved ones so dear …

Yet I had nothing,
for I had not my King.
To guide and direct me,
in everything.

I had not His peace
to fill me within.
I had no real faith,
in a world full of sin.

Daily I awoke,
with a sad heavy heart.
Drudging through the day,
wishing it to never start.

My heart would cry out,
so heavy with tears.
I wondered so often—
"Why was I here?"

There was a longing,
deep down in my soul.
I searched and I searched,
for answer's untold.

I prayed and I prayed.
One day I broke through.
I sent up a prayer.
"Please fill me with Truth."

"Oh precious Father,
from heaven above.
I've heard all about
your unending love.

I've heard You bring joy,
where sadness now lives.
I've heard You sent Jesus,
to wash away my sins.

I've heard of a home
You're preparing for me.
All I need do
is trust and believe.

You've knocked on the door
of my heart in the past.
So here now my Jesus,
it's opened at last.

Please come in.
Be my Lord and my King.
Here is my heart,
my everything."

The moment I prayed,
this short simple prayer.
The Father of light,
shined His light everywhere.

Where once there was darkness.
Now I could see.
Where once there was pain.
He brought healing to me.

Where once there was sadness.
Now there's great joy.
Where once there was sin.
Now there's grace and much more.

Where once there was doubt.
I have faith in my Lord.
Where once there was fear.
I have peace evermore.

Though life may bring pain,
I cannot see.
I walk not alone.
It's now Jesus and me ...

June 29, 2004

Almost

You've brought me through the fire again,
   like so many times before.
Why do I worry and fret so, Lord,
   when trials knock at my door?

I have to laugh a little, Lord,
   You know this one was long—
But Oh! The lessons I have learned,
   they really make me strong.

I guess You laughed a little too,
   as You heard me scream and howl.
Seeing that You knew the end—
   I only know the now.

So I'll not worry and fret now, Lord,
   as trials come to my door—
Almost makes me want to cry,
   "Please, Father, give me more!"

An Outreached Hand

You took me in not knowing me;
   as a friend, as a sister you treated me.
For this I am truly thankful ...

You looked not upon my sin to judge me,
   but to love me;
For this I am truly grateful ...

You accepted me on level ground
   not putting yourselves higher than me;
For this I know is a great gift ...

You sacrificed yourselves and your needs
   at a time I so desperately needed you and your strength;
For this I bless you ...

You have given to me a new hope, a rekindle in my spirit,
   a desire to look up once again and say I can
and I will go forward with You, God.
For this I praise my Father ...

You were yourselves,
   just as God intended us to be;
For this I THANK YOU!

Love in Christ
Freda Westnedge

Another Love Letter

Father, have I told You lately,
    just how much I care?
Please accept my "Thank You"
    for always being there.

Have I told You that You are,
    my closest, very best friend?
Your love for me is breathless,
    there's no beginning—no end.

Have I said "I love You"
    other than in a prayer?
Let me tell it to You now,
    as we share this ocean air.

I love Your created beauty,
    the mountains stretching high—
The vastness of the ocean,
    the blue-tint crystal sky.

The water's cleansing power,
    as the sound rushes through my soul—
I feel so clean and fresh my God,
    as the waves break forth and roll.

I love Your gentle Spirit,
    He guides me every day.
He comforts me in sadness,
    He takes my pain away.

He tells me all about You,
   He helps me know You more.
He teaches me to honor You
   as Father and as Lord.

He gives me strength when I am weak,
   He helps me battle the night.
He gives me power through Your word,
   to fight this spiritual fight.

I love You both, dear Father God,
   the two of You are one—
You sent Him to me on this earth,
   after You took Your Son.

And speaking of Your Son, now Lord,
   I love Him most of all—
'Cause He saved me from death and hell,
   my ransom from the fall.

Jesus, my sweet Jesus,
   You bled and died for me—
You took my place upon the tree,
   when You died on Calvary.

Oh! But the story's not ended,
   for the Victory was Your own—
You have a place with the Father,
   sitting on the right of His throne.

I love You Father, Spirit, and Son,
   for the three of You are one—
I'll see You face to face someday,
   when my work on earth is done …

Back Home

How sweet this is
The calmness of the night
And to feel the great presence
Of my Savior tonight
The stars are so lovely
The lights are so bright
Within my heart sings
A melody this night
Of the love and the grace
That You've brought to my life
No greater joy, Lord
Ever have I known
Than that special day
When I knew I was home
Back home to You now
My heavenly King
Never again to go back
From whence I came.

Blessings

I pray a special blessing, Lord,
   upon my sister today.
I pray that You would meet her needs,
   in each and every way.

I pray that You would give to her,
   the desires of her heart;
For speaking forth Your word, dear Lord,
   she sure does do her part.

I pray You'd give to her Dear Lord,
   great riches from above.
I thank You for her wisdom,
   and unconditional love.

I pray You'd bring her son back home,
   to the fold where he belongs.
Bless her home with peacefulness;
   give her heavenly songs.

I pray that You remind her, Lord,
   of past victories she's won;
So she will see Your faithfulness,
   as she's prayed YOUR WILL BE DONE.

I pray You give her husband, Lord,
   Godly wisdom too …
I pray their love be strong and pure;
   FOR THEIR FAITH IS FOUND IN YOU …

Blood Red

Today, Lord, I made paper roses,
So lovely in color were they.
Some yellow, some pink, red, and some white—
They each had a message to say.
The white one, a message of purity—
Am I pure, Lord, in Your eyes today?
The yellow one signifies friendship—
Have I been friendly as I've gone on my way?
The pink sends a message of passion—
How great Lord was Your passion for me.
How, oh Lord, could I repay You—
For the gift of eternity.
The red one as You know, Lord,
Is symbolic of love—
So deep in color it reminds me of blood—
Could that be the reason its message is love?

Bringing Hope

I knelt beside the young mother,
I listened as she spoke …
Her eyes were red from crying,
she said her heart was broke …

I searched within my spirit,
words of comfort, I needed to share …
I recognized her pain that day—
I too, have been there …

The angels came one morning,
it was a bright and sunny day …
They took the hand of my mother,
and gently lead her away …

I know they took her to heaven,
I know she's with the Lord …
As a young and innocent child,
she opened up that door …

She had a friend in Jesus,
she shared His love with me …
She showed me by example,
how faithful He would be …

So through the pain that I had walked,
I gave this mother hope …
I held her in my arms real tight,
I whispered—"Jesus, will help you cope."

Just let the rivers of tears flow free,
be honest, He knows your heart …
The grief is just a process,
the healing, now will start …

Just curl up in His loving arms,
He's as gentle as a dove …
Rest now child, for you are safe,
in the Father's precious love …

Written March 20, 2002

Burdens for the Lost

I'll sit before you,
   till day becomes dawn.
I want to feel you,
   in my heart—in my song.

There's no greater joy,
   in my heart, Lord, today;
Than wanting your will—
   where to go—what to say.

The Harvest is white,
   the fields, they are plenty.
Oh! Precious souls,
   they are waiting—they are ready.

Move me and stir me,
   renew my heart to compassion.
Fill me with love,
   that spurs me to action.

Let not my feet
   rest in the day—
Until I have spoken,
   the words that You say.

Flood my lips,
   with your anointing power—
Bid me to go Father,
   for haste is the hour.

To minister, to serve,
   to weep with the sad—
To comfort in death,
   rejoice with the glad.

There's so many jobs
   for your people to do.
Refresh me now, Lord—
   make my burden anew ...

Can I Ask Why?

I'm humbled today as I think of You, Lord,
And the love you have shown to me ...
Though I don't understand, how this fits in your plan—
I'm here again, Lord, on my knees ...

With a heart that is heavy, I come to Thee—
Deep within my pillow I cry ...
I pour out my questions, I lift up my pain—
As my broken heart yearns to know why?

I try to walk by faith—though I stumble—
I try not to walk by sight ...
Oh Lord, it's so difficult—As You know—
Dear Jesus, am I losing the fight?

I know I am weak, my Father.
The battle scars run very deep ...
At times I get so frightened—
At times, Lord, I cannot sleep ...

I lift up my head toward heaven—
I know, Lord, You are there ...
I know, Lord, You are listening—
I know You have heard my prayer ...

Carry Me[*]

A flicker of light
Comes faintly through;
God, why do I feel
So distant from You?

My head is spinning
My heart is pounding
My words seem empty
So unsounding

I cry mercy Father,
Have Mercy on me
Today I'm so weak,
Will You please carry me?

---

[*] Titled by Family

Children's Choir[*]

Remembering Christmas
Through the eyes of a child
The new fallen snow
So nippy yet mild
The twinkling lights
On the tree bright and gay
To remind us all
Of our Savior's Birthday
Christmas carols ringing
In our ears soft and sweet
As our children perform
To bring us a treat
They're not very big
But their hearts are so warm
Each Mom and Dad prays
To them come no harm
They've practiced so hard
For this special day
They'll sing up a storm
In their own little way
So now settle back
Relax and enjoy
While we feast from the songs
Of each girl and boy!

---

[*] Titled by family

Christmas Prayer for You

May God *Bless* you richly,
throughout the coming year.
May He shine *His Love*,
on those you hold dear.

May He give you *Peace*,
should storm clouds appear.
May He send His *Angels*,
to hold you near.

May He give you *Wisdom*,
when decisions come your way.
May He give you *Guidance*,
throughout your busy day.

May He give you *Hope*,
if despair should arise
and hold you close,
when tears fill your eyes.

May He walk there beside you,
where I cannot be.
May you hear Him whisper—
"My child, you mean the world to Me."

Come, Lord

Come quickly, Lord,
　I pray You will;
Come today,
　　while I am still.

Come while I
　can hear Your voice,
am not walking,
　　in my own resource.

Come while I
　am seeking Your face;
Come while I
　am running the race.

Come while I
　am serving You;
Come Lord Jesus,
　　and make it soon …

Daddy, Did You See Me?

Daddy, did you see me
as I stood there by your bed?
Could you feel me, Daddy
as I stroked your precious head?

Could you see me, Daddy
although your eyes were closed?
Could you see me standing there?
I stayed so very close.

Daddy, could you see the tears
running down my face?
I could not handle the pain inside,
as I walked into that place.

Could you feel me, Daddy
holding your hand so tight?
My heart was wishing I could say,
"Everything will be alright."

Did you hear me call your name?
I said, "Daddy, please don't go …
I love you so much, Daddy,
Oh, how I hope you know."

Were you dreaming, Daddy
of the good times that we shared?
The fun we had while fishing
out in the ocean air.

I thought about you all day long,
while at the beach today.
It brought back special memories
of family time at play.

Easter Egg hunts we had on the beach.
Picnics at the state park.
Friends and family all gathered there.
We played until it was dark.

You and I sure loved the beach,
we loved the salty air.
Daddy, when I get to heaven,
can we play again up there?

Somehow, Daddy, I think you knew
I was standing by your side.
I believe in my heart you were there,
as we said our "final goodbye."

So, *Happy Birthday Daddy*,
it's been a little over a year;
Since you moved to heaven,
we sure do miss you here ...

Written March 23, 2005

Drenched in Love[*]

You're in my thoughts
You're on my mind
I pray for you
Most all the time
I'm praying that
Our Father above
Will drench you with
His precious *Love*!

* Titled by family

Don't Wait

Don't put it off till tomorrow,
   please tell them you love them today.
You don't know when the Lord will call,
   you're not promised another day.

Especially if there's been some words,
   you just wish hadn't been said.
Drop your pride, humble yourself,
   don't wait till your loved one's dead.

I know that's not a very nice thought,
   we all want life to go on.
Yet we must face reality,
   this is today, yesterday is gone!

So think for a moment, how you could sow,
   the beauty of God's love;
Into the heart of someone special,
   someone you care a lot of.

I know if you will ask our God,
   ideas will flow like a flood.
Maybe a card, a quick phone call,
   or possibly a red rosebud?

He is the Father of love, our God,
   He knows just what we need.
So, dear friend, DON'T WAIT, I pray,
   get on a bended knee …

Dry Those Tears

Oh, precious ones,
   please don't cry.
I'm so happy here with Jesus.
   We're walking side by side.

He came last night with the angels.
   Oh, the singing was heavenly.
As He lifted me up I felt freedom,
   from my pain and agony ...

To be whole again and happy,
   no greater joy have I known.
He walked me down the streets of gold,
   saying, "Welcome, child, you're home."

He showed me what I've always wanted ...
   My mansion by the sea.
So precious loves, please don't cry.
   Wipe those tears for me.

Encouraging Retreat

There is a place I go every week,
I call it my "Encouraging Retreat."
A few of us ladies gather together,
we pray, we encourage, we receive.

We receive from each other, we receive from God's word,
we receive from the prayers that we reap.
Sometimes when we come, One's on the mountain,
another in a valley Oh so deep.

Sometimes I feel it the minute I hit the door—
This presence of God we've come to seek.
Other times it's when we start our sweet praise—
He's so faithful to meet us each week.

As the night starts unfolding, and the needs are all shared—
The love, the encouragement begin to flow.
Our hearts are united, our spirits are strong—
as we seek to understand and to grow.

To grow in the knowledge of our Lord Jesus Christ,
to grow in His strength and His love—
To grow in the belief as we open our hearts,
the true healing comes from our Father above.

It's encouraging to me as we meet week to week,
to see that, yes, we have grown.
We've fought many battles, we've walked through many storms—
But we all know that God's on the throne!

January 20, 1997, 06:30 a.m.

Experience Through Pain

Afflictions, trials, tribulations, and suffering,
    it's hard to put up with the pain—
However, I've learnt to trust You more,
    for closeness to You I have gained.

I speak not for others, only for myself,
    it brings me to my knees.
Acknowledging my weakness, confessing my need—
    relying on your strength indeed.

Each time I would cry out,
    Oh! God, please no more—
It seemed straight from heaven,
    You entered my door.

A cocoon of love
    wrapped around me so tight—
Your presence renews hope,
    my darkness turns to light.

I've learned like my brother,
    in the Word who's named Paul—
That through tribulations,
    I grow strong—I stand tall.

I learn I can praise you
    through heartache with a song—
I learn through the pain,
    in your arms I belong.

You teach me in the good times,
    You teach me in the bad—
You teach me when I'm happy,
    You teach me when I sad.

You've taught me to trust,
    all things work for my good—
Without the experience,
    how could I know that it would ...

Extraordinary Grace

I've tasted God's *Extraordinary Grace* ...
    I have felt His loving touch ...
I've fallen on my face before Him ...
    Oh! His mercy means so much!

His arms stretched open wide before me ...
    I wanted to hide ... I wanted to run ...
He said, "My child, I love you,
    I know what you have done."

"You cannot hide from me dear one,
    You cannot run away ..."
He said, "My love is unconditional,
    It will always be that way."

I knew His heart was hurting,
    When He saw me fall into sin ...
The tears fell from my eyes like rain ...
    When I humbled myself before Him ...

It hurt so much ... The pain I had caused ...
    To my Lord ... My Savior ... My Friend
Then I felt His warm embrace ...
    Of forgiveness ... once again ...

Written August 28, 2000

Far Away Friends

Friends past
   they last;
God connects the heart,
   they never, ever part.

Miles between,
   they never seem;
To keep the love,
   from strengthening.

Special moments
   linger on;
Reflecting times,
   to think upon.

My heart's the window,
   of times gone by;
The sweet embraces
   of you and I.

But friends
   in past,
they'll always last.

I love you still,
   I always will …

Father of Heaven[*]

Oh Father of heaven and of earth
I want to live up there
I want to hear You say to me
Come meet me in the air.
Oh Father of heaven and of earth
I want to hear You say
Well done thou good and faithful one
To others you've shown the way.
Oh Father of heaven and of earth
I want to hear You say
Come my child, beside me here
A crown for you today.
Oh Father of heaven and of earth
I want to hear You say
I've watched you as you've grown
I've led you all the way.
Come sit beside me now, my child
You have eternal life
You gave to me your all and all
You gave to me your life.

<hr>

*   Titled by family

Finding Our Home

I saw a little dog today,
   running down the road;
looking for this home of love,
   not knowing where to go.

I felt that little doggie's pain,
   the fear he had inside;
I've had the same within my life,
   sometimes I'd want to hide.

He ran up to some little boys,
   and sniffed them very well;
he thought for sure they'd be the ones,
   but no familiar smell.

The anguish I saw upon his face,
   I've seen throughout the world;
people passing hurriedly by,
   their lives all in a whirl.

I prayed for the little dog today,
   please, Lord, show him the way;
just like I pray for souls now lost,
   that this will be the day.

For them to say I need You, God,
   I've lost my pathway home;
direct me now with your light of love,
   and lead me where I belong.

We need not wait till we are lost,
  outrunning on our own;
the Father's hand is reaching out,
  "My child, I'll lead you home."

Food for My Soul[*]

When you're feeling
Down and blue
Here's the thing
That you must do

Lift your voice
And let it ring
Praises to our
Heavenly King

For when you sing
Your praise to Him
You will feel
The Spirit within

Begin to rise up
And be strong
Because the praise
To Him belongs

And it edifies
Deep in our soul
Brings us peace
And makes us whole

---

[*] Titled by family

Forever Close

I thought of you again today ...
I could see your precious smile;
As I gazed into your big brown eyes—
my heart longed, to talk for a while ...

I heard your laughter,
we so often shared.
I can hear it now—
ringing through the air ...

I remember your HUGS,
your strong embrace—
The warmth I felt—
may it never erase ...

I miss your phone calls,
late at night—
as you called to tell me—
"Everything's all right."

I miss you sharing,
what was on your heart ...
It never took long,
for the laughter to start ...

I remember as a child,
you would run to me—
with outstretched arms,
I placed you on my knee ...

You brought such joy
to my heart, even then …
I can see you now,
in your little playpen …

You thought for a while,
I was your mother …
The bond we shared,
was sister and brother …

Oh, how I thank,
our Father above—
That I had you here,
for a while to love …

Though short it was,
the years we had …
I'm eternally grateful—
I'm eternally glad …

Having you in my life,
was truly a blessing …
You're in God's arms now—
Eternally resting …

October 17, 2002

Mom wrote this poem about a year after her brother Timmy passed away. They were very close, and she was still grieving.

Forever Loving

At times I don't listen
   when you're speaking to me;
At times I even choose
   your face not to seek.

I give up the blessings
   You have for me in store;
By choosing purposely
   to ignore your knock on my door.

It's not that I don't love You,
   'cause, Lord, You know I do!
I just get so weak
   and my flesh comes fighting through.

It's at those times, Lord,
   your love I feel so strong;
Even when I'm weak
   and my choices are wrong.

You're always there
   waiting patiently for me;
Knowing that soon
   your face again I'll seek.

You bring no condemnation
   for my slips and my falls;
You're waiting to hear,
   your name when I call.

And lovingly You place
   your arms once again;
Around my heart
   and the healing begins …

Forever Reaching

My heart is forever
   reaching out to you.
No matter how often I stumble
   or feel kinda blue.

It's feeling kinda lost
   sadden with despair.
My prayers seem to be floating
   somewhere in midair.

My heart's great desire
   is to walk closer with you.
My precious Father
   please help me follow through.

Friendship[*]

There's nothing better on this earth
that I know …
Than the friendship, love
and caring you show …

When God's at the center
of our lives, as He is …
Friendship doesn't get
any better than this …

Written May 2003

Friendship Wings

My "dolly" friend
You've always been
There for me
Through thick or thin.

No matter how sad
My heart would be
You lifted me up
On "Friendship Wings"

Freda Westnedge
July 1, 2003
Written for one of her friends, from the online "Dolly" board.

Garment of Praise

Let me put
    on the garment of praise
whenever I'm burdened
    and my mind is in a daze.

Remind me of songs
    once sang unto you
and how they lift me—
    makes my spirit renewed.

'Tis then I can handle
    this world with its snares,
just knowing that Jesus—
    my God really cares …

Gifts from the Heart

Secret sisters, that's what we've been
   throughout the months gone past.
We've built a special friendship,
   I know will always last.

As I walked inside the church,
   upon a shelf I'd see;
A beautiful gift-wrapped package—
   I knew it was for me.

It came to me with lots of love,
   especially from you.
No matter what I'd find inside,
   I felt your heart there too.

Giving from the heart my friend
   it is the very best way.
Everyday a prayer went up
   and this is what I'd say.

Father, bless this friend of mine,
   in everything she'll do;
Bless her when she goes to sleep
   and with morning light anew.

Bless her as she goes about
   her daily morning task;
Give to her all good things—
   which she may humbly ask.

Bless her with the gifts You give
   to us that are now free;
Because she has a special love
   tucked in her heart for Thee.

Bless her loved ones and her home,
   bless her children too;
Bless the work that she may do,
   in service unto you.

Tonight I'll find out who You are;
   It will not matter you see—
'Cause we share a very special bond—
   'Tis Jesus, You and Me …

Give It to Jesus

The pain, like a knife,
    went straight to my heart;
As I listened to the burden
    that was tearing her apart.

As she cried I could feel,
    the tears on my face.
A wish for the moment—
    to have taken her place.

To lift her pain,
    that cut to the core—
At least I could tell her—
    "That's what Jesus is for."

Our barrier of grief,
    burdens too heavy to carry;
We roll them on Him,
    and in "His" presence we tarry.

Giving

Do something for someone else today,
  ask God to guide your way;
And from the blessing they receive,
  You will have been repaid.

For giving of ourselves to others,
  is the greatest gift of all;
For it was when the Father spoke,
  that Jesus answered the call.

For had He not been willing,
  to give himself for us;
Where would we be today my friend?
  we all would be so LOST!

By reaching out to others,
  God blesses us through them;
For when we give ourselves away,
  WE FIND OURSELVES IN HIM!

Go Sweet Spirit

I've learned to take You
   at your word,
when in my heart
   from You I've heard.

I've learned You do not
   lie to me;
when You speak,
   your will I seek.

That I may walk
   with You in power,
going forth
   this final hour;

Praying now
   so earnestly
that You answer
   speedily;

My petition
   to your throne,
for my loved ones—
   please bring them home.

Send your angels
   to their sides,
to keep them safe,
   till they reply;

To your call
    within their hearts;
Go Sweet Spirit
    and do your part.

Draw them to
    our King of kings,
help them come
    on bended knees.

Renew their hearts
    of stone and clay,
hurry now,
    oh! Don't delay …

Let them hear Him
    at the door,
give new faith
    and trust restore.

Your word has promised
    this to me;
Go Sweet Spirit
    and set them free …

God is Near

Flowers, trees,
birds everywhere—
Bringing whispers of spring
floating in the air ...

Folks out walking,
children at play—
Warms my heart,
on this bright sunny day ...

Rivers of water,
So blue, so clear ...
All nestled together,
God is near ...

Written March 31, 2004

God's Blessings

Be thankful all ye people,
   for what God has done for you.
He has rolled back the clouds of heaven,
   to send His blessings flowing through.

He has given of His grace,
   so rich and abundantly,
and poured into our hearts His love,
   so sweet and tenderly.

He gave to us His only son,
   He showed the world He cared.
He took Him from His throne on high,
   that He alone had shared.

For sinners just like you and me,
   He shed His precious blood,
so we may be redeemed of God,
   to share His home above.

He gave us understanding,
   that we would someday know,
the depth within His mercy,
   to others He will show.

Forgiveness is a blessing,
   no one should reject.
He gives to us so freely,
   just pray, believe, accept.

And last, but surely not the least,
   the greatest of them all,
the precious Holy Spirit,
   He is for one and all!

Grace Carried Me

How did I drift from you,
my precious Lord?
How did I walk
so far from your door?

When did it start,
the slow change of mind?
I know it was not
a short space of time.

One thought over here,
another one there;
Before I knew it
the father of err—

Was whispering sweet words
so enticing to me,
Why didn't I run?
Why didn't I scream?

I know that I fought
for a period of time,
But I was so weak,
deceived and so blind.

There was a crack in my armor—
missing fellowship too;
So many adjustments,
in this place that was new.

I know that your word
spoke truth from the start,
But I justified
every word in my heart.

The pain was so deep,
I couldn't fight anymore;
My strength was so drained,
from the "Spiritual War."

It's been a long haul,
now my healing's complete—
I'm back home in your arms,
sitting at your feet.

One thing You taught me,
as I fell to the floor—
Where sin does abound,
there's *Grace* all the more!

Grandmother[*]

Thank You, Lord
My prayer has come true
I'll be a grandmother
Thanks to You

A bundle of joy
To hold real tight
To squeeze and love
With sheer delight

Another life
To give my love to
A special love
that comes from only You

An abundance of pride
Has filled my heart
As I pray to You
That I'll do my part

To guide this little one
To the Tree of Life
And be an example
Of Your burning Light

So let Your light
Shine out from me
That this dear little one
May see my love for Thee!

---

[*] Titled by Family

Guard My Tongue

Jesus, please forgive me today—
    Your light was a little dim.
I know my husband did not see,
    Your love as I looked at him.

My heart was heavy, the pain was deep—
    as the conversation began,
I knew I should have took the time—
    to bend my knee and repent.

The flesh is quick to demand its way,
    no warning does it give—
It lashes out, its venom spew—
    you wish you could relive.

I thank You for your Spirit, Lord,
    Your loving, correcting hand—
I thank You that You spoke to me—
    "Be gentle with this man."

When he looks into my eyes,
    dear Jesus, let him see—
Your tender mercy, wrapped in love—
    flowing out of me.

Thank You, Jesus,
Your daughter, Freda

Guide Me[*]

Guide me, Lord
Give me your strength
Help me to walk
In your loving footprints
Teach me your ways
Help me each day
To know what to do
To know what to say
To know when to go
To know when to stay
Guide me by night
Guide me by day!

Happy Birthday, Daddy, How's Heaven Today?

Hello, Daddy,
How are you today?
Are the golden streets of heaven
As beautiful as they say?
I imagine the face of Jesus
Is shining all about
I hear You and Mother are singing
Sweet praises to Him with a shout.
Today's your birthday, Daddy,
I've been pretty sad
When I think of where you are,
This sad heart turns to glad.
I've been missing Timmy, Daddy,
His birthday's coming soon
I think of him so often
Morning, night, and noon.
I hope they give you a heavenly party,
We have a lot of family there
I know how much they love you
I know how much they care.
Please give them all a kiss for me
Tell them I love them so
I'll meet you all up there someday
When it's time for me to go.
I'm thankful for the hope we have
Without it I'd surely die
Because of Jesus we'll meet again
In our heavenly home in the sky.

So happy birthday, Daddy
I still love you very much
Our hearts are still connected
And I'll be keeping in touch.

May 19, 2004

*Happy Birthday, Friend**

Happy, happy birthday,
my sweet and special friend ...
I pray it's filled with laughter,
until the very end ...

I pray for you, the sunshine,
to warm and light your way ...
I pray for God's protection,
throughout your "special" day ...

I pray for smiles upon your face,
for joy to fill your heart ...
I pray that friends and loved ones,
surround you from the start ...

But most of all, I pray for you,
our Lord and Master's touch ...
Because my very special friend,
He loves you very much ...

God bless you, Joan, I love you ... Freda

Written January 26, 2002

---

* Titled by family

*Hard Trials**

Deep valleys … Hard Trials,
   They come and they go;
We learn to plant … We learn to sow.

We learn that pain
   brings forth the good …
We grow in strength
   as He said we would …

Written January 27, 1987

*   Titled by family

He Comforts Me

Blessed are the mourners, for they shall be comforted,
    this is my Father's words to me.
So I shall hold my head up high—
    for someday His face I'll see.

My trial may be so heavy now,
    that I feel I cannot bear.
I know while in my darkest hour—
    my Father's love is there.

I know He feels my pain inside,
    He hurts with every tear.
I know not what tomorrow brings—
    He whispers, "Do not fear."

He says my child, I'll walk with you,
    I'll hold your hand so tight.
Together we will make it through,
    this lonely darkened night.

The burdens that you bear, my child,
    are there to make you strong.
You'll come shining through the fire—
    because to me you belong.

With the dawning of the new day,
    your spirit I will renew.
I have just one last word my child—
    "Remember, I'm always with you."

He Gave

I deserved Death—
  He gave me Life.

I deserved Hell—
  He gave me Heaven.

I deserved Condemnation—
  He gave me None.

I deserved Sickness—
  He gave me Health.

I deserved Poverty—
  He gave me Riches.

I deserved spiritual Darkness—
  He gave me Light.

I deserved Blindness—
  He opened my Eyes.

I deserved Hate—
  He gave me Love.

I deserved no Good Thing—
  He gave me Everything!

He Hears My Heart

I love to talk to the Father,
   I love to talk to the Son …
I love to talk to the Trinity,
   the mighty three in one …

I love to lift my heart to them,
   sharing how my day has been …
Lifting hands to magnify,
   giving praise to God on high …

I always know that He'll be there,
   I'm not just talking to the air …
He listens with His heart of love—
   answers me from up above …

My tears are never shed in vain,
   for my Father knows my pain …
He never, ever judges me,
   gives His love and forgiveness "Free" …

I know that He's my only hope …
   Without Him I just could not cope …
I love to talk to the Father, I love to talk to the Son …
   I love to talk to the Trinity—The Mighty Three in One …

Written March 29, 2001

He is Light

Oh Lord, who is light but You.
   You spoke the light of my day
into existence, giving me hope
   in place of despair.

You shined Your love into my heart
   revealing to me my need for You.
You light up my spirit
   with Your love.

Your word is a lamp unto my feet
   which guides my path
into the direction
   You have for me to walk.

Where could I be
   without You, my God—
Your long arm of mercy reached down
   and brought me out of deception …

How can I ever repay You?
   I will follow You all the days of my life—
I will be Your daughter
   and You will be my Father.

Your love is good
   and perfect—
From everlasting to everlasting—
   Unconditional and free.

How great is your love for me
   Oh God!
And I want to say to You—
   I love You from the depth of my heart …

Lovingly Your Daughter,
Freda

He Loves Me

I've often thought You cared for others,
  a little more than You cared for me.
But, OH dear God, how wrong I was!
  That lie no longer will I receive.

You're no respecter of persons,
  the requirement for all is the same;
All that anyone has to do,
  is believe upon your name.

You've proved your love for me so often,
  now I can finally see;
Without a doubt, I know for sure …
  You really do love me!

He Understands

Even in the valleys
  I know you're by my side …
Even though I'd rather be
  on mountains stretching high.

In times like these
  I know that I
need to walk by faith—
  Not by sight.

As darken clouds
  roll over my soul;
I know, my God
  you're in control.

I know that you
  still hold my hand …
I know, my Lord,
  You understand …

November 8, 2004

He Waits for Me

I will come before the Lord in praise.
    I will lift up my heart unto Him.
Him only will I give my whole heart.
    To my God I pour out my prayers.

My God hears every word I whisper.
    He waits for me in the morning.
He waits to hear me speak.
    He waits to enfold me in His love.

My God wants to show me His mercy.
    His desire is to lift my spirit.
He wants to bring me into His presence.
    He desires my attention.

He basks in the praises of my lips.
    His heart swells with pride
as I sing Him love songs
    from my heart.

He is my Father, I am His child.
    His long suffering to me is great.
His forgiveness fills my heart to overflowing.
    The beauty I feel as I stand in His presence is awesome.

His love for me is everlasting.
    I will Praise my King until my breath has ceased.
I will Praise my Father as long as I have my being.
    He delights in my Praises.

In Him alone will I place my trust.

    He is worthy of my Praises.

He is worthy of my love.

    Oh so worthy of my Praises, oh so worthy of my love.

March 23, 2005

Healing Love

I wish, dear Lord, I could write of Your love
    and the impact You've had on my life.
The grace and mercy You've given to me,
    the victories through "spiritual fights."

The times that Your hands,
    so gentle and kind
have held me and rocked me
    till I received peace of mind.

I remember when I was just a little girl,
    I ran to Your altar of love—
Reached out to You with eyes full of tears—
    You promised a home up above.

I remember how lonely I felt through those years—
    confused, rejected, unloved;
But You always whispered an encouraging word—
    "I love You with an everlasting love!"

Though Father and Mother reject me, oh Lord,
    You never turned a deaf ear—
You watched me grow and guided my steps—
    You stayed so very near.

You saw all my pain, You wiped all my tears,
    You walked with me through fear and through shame.
You never left me, year after year—
    You taught me to call on your name.

So now, dear Lord, I release all the pain,
    I experienced in those tender young years—
Lift them to You, who's faithful and true,
    You've given "beauty" for ashes and "joy" for tears.

You've promised me, Lord, that death nor life
    nor principalities,
could separate me from your love—
    from now till eternity …

Healing through Forgiveness

Forgiveness crying
    from the depth of me,
Oh! The pain,
    the agony;

No! No!,
    why must it be?
It was you who caused
    the hurt in me.

Healing come,
    Oh! Wholeness I plea,
I want to be free,
    from this aching in me.

Anger, sweet anger,
    I must look at you too;
I now realize,
    yes, I do have you.

Oh! Come, sweet Spirit,
    Sweet Spirit, be not slow;
Come and heal me,
    of this pain that you know;

Its wounded and scarred
    and left ugly marks;
Gone deep in my soul,
    penetrated my heart.

Help me forgive,
  give me strength to forget,
Don't let me deny
  but now may I let;

You walk me so gently,
  to your healing shore,
I'm ready once more
  to open the door;

Come pour unto
  my heart once again,
Your ANOINTING OINTMENT,
  let your healing begin …

Heart of a Friend

Friendship is
a connection of hearts.
The bonded feeling
you get from the start.

It's that feeling of knowing
that your secrets within—
Are tucked in the heart
of your true loyal friend.

It's that confident feeling
you're accepted as you—
Even if you've had
a bad day or feel blue.

It's knowing that you have
her unconditional love—
That was sent from the Father
in heaven above.

More important, it's days
when you two are apart—
You feel her friendship—
and it warms your heart.

Heartache of Rejection

Anger cuts deep into my spirit,
as the rejection races across his face.
The insensitivity shown, through the man I love,
brings heartache that is hard to erase.

Oh, God, I hate this part of me,
that allows the hurt to go deep.
Help me lift it now to you—
it's your "forgiveness" I want to reap.

Thank You, Lord …

Heaven's Growing Sweeter

My heart is yearning
For heaven's door
My heart is yearning
For my precious Lord
I want to see His beautiful face
I want to feel His warm embrace
I want to see my loved ones there
I want to stroke my mother's hair
I want to tell her
I miss her so
My love for her
Has not grown cold
I think of her so much
Each day
How I wish she hadn't
Gone away
Yet now it makes
Heaven much sweeter
'Cause Jesus and Mother
Will be my greeter.

Heavenly Angels

Once I was told
   I had an hour to live.
I met the "Great Physician,"
   new life He did give.

I once heard the angels
   singing their song.
They were declaring the glory
   of God on the throne.

They were singing of His coming,
   with *Great Power* and *Might*.
My heart is yearning,
   for that glorious sight.

Twice I had an angel
   intervene on my behalf.
A dangerous car
   was taken right out of my path.

Actually I know
   there's been more along the way,
As I've prayed for protection
   for my family each day.

Once I met a stranger
   and spoke of the Lord.
What a privilege—they received Him
   and experienced great joy.

My dog ran away
  in a thunderstorm.
My heart was so heavy
  broken and torn.

My faith was growing weak,
  the time had been long.
But my little girl believed—
  her faith remained strong.

Yes, of course,
  He brought her back home.
In the arms of my daughter—
  is where Heidi belonged.

Once I needed ice,
  I believed and received—
Could God really care
  of such a simple of need?

You betcha my friend
  even the simplest of prayers,
Are answered of the Father,
  as we breathe them in prayer.

There's been many more
  as I've walked this great path,
But none will compare—
  to seeing Jesus at last.

As I fall to my knees
  to worship my King,
Nothing will matter—
  as before Him I sing.

I'll dance and I'll shout,
  I'll give Him all praise.
I'll thank Him for saving me
  and guiding me each day.

I'll thank Him for placing
  His angels in my care—
I have so much to share,
  with my Jesus up there ...

Heavenly Messengers

I heard the angels sing tonight
They captured my heart in song
Sweet praises singing to our Lord
All glory and honor belong

A heavenly wind, the flutter of wings
As they filled the room in flight
Love was ringing in the air
Oh, what a glorious sight

"Hearken unto Him", they called
"Behold your Heavenly King."
"He's coming soon with Power and Love."
Sing, sweet angels, sing!

He'll be There

I cannot be everything to you,
    nor turn your gray skies into blue.
I cannot hold your heart every day,
    nor make your burdens all vanish away.

I cannot wipe each and every tear
    that you have cried throughout the year.
I cannot take your pain away
    that you are feeling this very day.

What I can and will do friend,
    is give you hope that your pain will end.
I've walked your road, each and every step,
    my heart was broken, my eyes had wept.

Then I met this friend of mine,
    He seemed to come in the nick of time.
He knew everything I was crying for
    'cause He'd been down this road before.

He asked me to take hold of "His" hand—
    somehow I knew "He" could understand.
Now my skies, which once were gray
    are a brilliant blue, 'cause "He" came that day.

I had to open
    the door for "Him"
I had to ask—
    "Jesus Please Come In."

His Beauty

Walking amongst the flowers,
I see Him there.
Gazing upon the mountain high,
His beauty is everywhere.
Waves breaking on a sandy beach,
The wind softly on my face.
I'm overcome with His beauty,
I'm saturated by His Grace.
I feel His love in a baby's smile,
Or a friend who takes my hand.
Forever I'm blessed to call Him Lord,
To be part of his plan.

Written May 22, 2005

His Grace

How my soul does cry for thee,
for my God of Calvary,
    for that place of rest and peace,
that heaven above you've prepared for me.
How I long to see the face,
of the one whose grace does save,
me from the world and all its snares,
Oh, my God, how much You care.

His Presence

You have given me,
   Hope, Peace, and Love.
Not questioning why,
   I just accept.

You have given me,
   Life, Happiness, and overflowing Joy.
Not trying to repay,
   I just receive.

You have given me,
   Healing, Restoration, Forgiveness.
For this I am,
   Eternally Grateful.

You have helped me to see,
   that life in abundance,
is not what the world
   has to offer me.

You have given to me,
   a new dimension of love,
not what I perceive love to be
   but what it is in reality.

This love of yours is quite encompassing;
   never judging, never stumbling,
never finding fault within,
   does not condemn me when I sin.

You have given me heaven, through,
   this time on earth I spend with you …

His Presence in the Night

I know it's late, my Father,
    but please be patient with me;
I've just got to write about this love!
    It's way deep inside, You see.

I don't know how to describe it,
    I feel I want to sing;
I want to shout to the whole wide world,
    about this love You bring.

I feel so special, all aglow inside,
    I feel your presence so near.
How precious is your love, dear God,
    how sweet your voice I hear.

Oh, the love You have for me,
    such love I don't deserve;
Yet you give to me so freely—
    Oh Father, it's You I'll serve.

I love You with my heart and soul,
    I love You with my mind;
You are so dear and sweet to me,
    My Father, You are so kind.

Although this love can never be told,
    it is too deep within;
I'll close with one last thought in mind—
    Thank You, Father, for cleansing me from all my sins …

Lovingly,
Your daughter, Freda

His Word

My eyes have seen
My ears have heard
Of many great miracles
In our Father's Word
It is a lifeline
To the dying soul
It offers peace
With riches untold
It gives direction
When all seems lost
It tells of Jesus
Who paid the cost
It protects me from
The world in err
And keeps me safe
From the devil's snare
It is a light
Unto my feet
A safe hiding place
In time of retreat
It gives me strength
To carry on
Through victories and battles
That I have won
It tells of a home
Where loved ones wait
Of streets of gold
And pearly gates
It tells of angels
Watching over me
And how my life
Should always be

A living sacrifice
To my King of kings
And out of my voice
His praise should ring
It tells me how
I should run the race
By keeping my eyes
Only on His face.

Home Away from Home

I'll meet you in the morning
We'll start our day with God
We'll open up our hearts to Him
And see just what He's got
He loves for us to seek His face
He loves for us to pray
He loves for us to take the time
To be with Him each day
He loves to speak to every heart
Each in a different way
Does someone need a Healing?
Maybe strength for your day?
He'll be right there for each of us
He loves us all, you see
So come right in and sit awhile
With Jesus, you and me
So come on in my sweet dear friends
Let's bow before His throne
We'll snuggle in this quiet room
Our home away from home.

Home Front*

Warm tears ran down my face today
I could not stop their flow
I feel a burden in my heart
For those I do not know
Miles away they're dying
In a land so far from home
Fighting for Our freedom
To say a prayer is all I know
I wish that I could be there
To hold their lonely hands
To give an encouraging word
But the "Home Front" is where I stand
I feel their pains of loneliness
For the loved ones they left behind
For the sleepless nights of sorrow
As they wrestle with their time
I wish that I could show them
My heartfelt gratitude
To offer up a word of "Thanks"
Would be the least that I could do
But I know my Father loves them
I place them in His hands
I'll offer up this simple prayer
"Father, send them comfort;
Give them strength to stand!"

---

* Finished and titled by family

I Saw a Life Slip Away Today

Today I saw a life slip by,
   on You, my Lord, did he rely?
Did You once call upon him, Lord?
   Did he respond, open up that door?

Life is so fragile
   yet in a moment's time,
You call our name
   we're next in line.

Sometimes we think
   it can't be me,
He must mean
   Bill, Ed, or Lee.

One more day
   I'm sure I have,
I'll clean things up
   it won't be so bad.

Then it's here
   you're next in line—
You wish you'd answered
   His call last time.

When so gently
   you heard Him speak—
Come my son
   kneel at my feet.

Let me give
　　you all the love,
your hearts been craving—
　　I'm your Father above.

Come now child
　　grab hold of my hand,
Accept my Son—
　　salvation's plan.

I sent Him here
　　to die for you,
Accept His blood—
　　have life renewed.

He is the way
　　the truth, the life—
You might not have
　　the time tonight.

For like my friend
　　you know not when,
His voice will shout—
　　you'll be ushered in.

So please don't wait
　　don't quench the call—
The Father says
　　come one come all …

I See

I see her running in green grassed meadows,
    I see her happy and gay;
I see her smiling face so clear,
    "I'm free" I hear her say.

No pain, no agony—now felt,
    sweet calm and peacefulness;
I see her take our Savior's hand,
    how sweet, he gave her a kiss.

I Shall Not Want

My confidence lies
   in You, my Lord.
I shall not want
   for anything more.

I shall not want
   for beauty untold,
I shall not want
   for riches and gold.

I shall not want
   a sweet word sublime,
as payment for
   my talent or time.

I shall always want
   the spirit so free,
flowing throughout my life
   and leading me.

I shall always want
   simplicity,
a bended knee
   and humility.

I shall always want
   to walk with you;
Please show me now
   what you'd have me do.

If I Could

I wish so much I could tell you,
How very special you are …
I wish that I could tell you,
The love that's in my heart …

As you sit in front of your computers—
Sending your love my way …
You've given to me the greatest gift—
You've lifted my spirits today …

As the gray clouds smothered the sunshine …
As the rain began to fall,
And the blue birds' song was muffled,
I felt your love most of all …

So if I could send you a rainbow,
I would plaster it across the sky …
If I could send you sunshine,
I would spread it far and wide …

If I could send my love to you …
I'd bottle it in a jar—
To let it spill all over you—
Going deep inside your heart …

Written October 18, 2002

Mom had so many cyberfriends! Most of them she had never met, but she "talked" to them all the time! She would send them her poems to encourage them, make and send them blankets to comfort them, and she was never afraid to tell them about her Jesus!

If Only They Knew

Father God, we need you
  and your Strength today.
Our Nation is suffering
  in a terrible way.

There's earthquakes, there's famine,
  there's fires, there's floods—
People are homeless,
  in the streets there's shed blood!

They're fighting, they're looting,
  they're running in fear—
They know that it's coming—
  that judgment is near.

The snow is so deep
  in parts of our world—
They're freezing, they're dying,
  their lives are in a whirl.

There's just so much heartache,
  it's hard to explain—
When asked how our God,
  could allow all this pain.

Oh! But If only,
  they knew, what we knew—
How all of these signs,
  say you're coming here soon.

If only they knew,
　　because of hardness of heart,
They've caused the disasters—
　　they've all done their part.

They've taken You out,
　　of our nation today—
Our children in school,
　　are not allowed to pray.

They scoff and they mock,
　　at the righteous and meek—
They kill unborn babies,
　　by the hundreds each week.

They worship the dollar,
　　teach that abstinence is wrong—
Their success is more important,
　　than family and home.

Men lie with men,
　　women do too—
Oh! Precious Father,
　　it's abomination to you.

You wish none to suffer,
　　that all would repent—
You made an escape,
　　when Jesus You sent.

But they think it's too simple,
　　a crutch to mankind—
Oh! How much longer,
　　will their eyes be so blind?

I know that You love us,
    though sinners we be—
The price has been paid
    by the blood on Calvary.

Jesus was payment
    You sent for us all—
Please help them to listen
    and heed to your call.

Our land You will heal,
    if we'll be humble and pray—
"Teach us, dear Father,
    to trust and obey!"

If You Should Remember

If you should remember a sin I've committed,
  don't bring it up to me …
I've brought it to the throne room of God—
  His grace has set me free …

If you should remember, a word I spoke,
  that broke your heart one day;
I want you to know it broke mine too,
  as I kneeled before the Lord to pray …

If you should remember a time you were sick,
  and I was too busy to care;
Please know I've asked for forgiveness—
  Next time, I'll try to be there …

Do you remember the time you were lonely?
  Your heart was broken in two?
God planted you into my heart that day—
  Gave a covenant friendship, to me and you …

I am not perfect, I don't claim to be;
  They'll be times I will let you down …
Remember, my friend, as we walk through this life—
  It's on "His love" we can count …

I pray you remember,
  only the good times we've shared—
My words spoken in love—
  The times I showed I cared …

For I only have this moment in time;
    Tomorrow's not promised to me—
I pray each day, Lord, help me to be,
    the woman you've created me to be …

Written March 14, 2002

I'll Be Away for a While

I'll be away for a little while ...
   you'll be in my heart.
Every time I think of you,
   my day will always start;

With a smile upon my face,
   you have put it there ...
Every time I think of you,
   my smile goes everywhere.

For you, my friends, mean more to me
   than words could ever express.
You make me laugh, sometimes cry,
   you bring me happiness.

So when I'm miles away from you
   I won't be lonely or sad ...
I'll think about my love for you,
   and all the fun we've had ...

That will hold me over
   until I see you again.
We'll have a lot to talk about,
   my precious cyberfriends.

Written June 1, 2004

I'm Hurting[*]

Father, I'm hurting within my soul
This dark, dark feeling, will You unfold
I want to run, I want to hide
Not face this pain, I'm feeling inside
It billows up into my throat
I choke back tears, and feel so cold
I feel rejection from my dear friend
It smothers Your love, and peace within
My mind's confused, I don't understand
I know Your healing, is the perfect plan
So now bring light, into my soul
Reveal to me, the bondage hold.

---

[*] Titled by family

In His Arms

Today if I could see
    the sand upon the beach;
One set of footprints
    is all there would be.

For this is a trial
    I cannot bear on my own;
He surely is carrying me—
    my Jesus alone.

My heart is so heavy,
    the hurt cuts so deep;
I cannot see daylight—
    my eyes only weep.

My true test of Faith—
    will I win at the end?
Only if I lean
    on my faithful best friend.

His suffering was great,
    His pain—much worse than mine.
But as He carried His cross,
    I was on His mind.

He already knew
    what this day would hold for me;
That's why He had to hang,
    on the tree at Calvary.

He won the victory
  so He could ease my pain.
I know when I come through—
  I'll be the winner—In His Name!

Written June 12, 1997

In His Presence

Sitting in your presence, I'm spellbound;
Like a sponge, I'm soaking up your love.

If feels like a warm summer's day
with the sun shining on my face.

I feel your caresses in my heart
as you are revealing your love to me.

I don't want to move from this room …
I feel as if I could sit here for hours.

Now that I KNOW you're there …
PRAISE GOD! I can handle anything …

In Search of Love

As I think back,
　　upon growing up;
There's only one dream,
　　I thought a lot of.

I always wanted
　　a close family;
With lots of love,
　　to understand me.

One to be myself with,
　　and give my love so free;
Who wouldn't expect me to be something,
　　that wasn't inside of me.

I tried so hard to find it.
　　I looked just everywhere.
I got into some worldly things,
　　surely I'd find it there!

I went along my merry way,
　　with happiness I thought;
Until I came to a dead end,
　　no inner peace was brought.

Then I remembered a word,
　　my brother spoke one year;
"Don't you know, my sister,
　　it comes not from the world we have here."

"It comes from our Heavenly Father,
    and he alone can give;
You all the love you've searched for,
    throughout the years you've lived."

He told me I needed repentance,
    and to be born again;
I could not understand it,
    but knew it was God's true plan.

I did as he suggested,
    and oh! the peace I felt;
And all the love I had searched for,
    while there before Jesus I knelt.

Now I am in God's family,
    with love that flows so free;
I have the great opportunity,
    to be the real and only me …

Inner Healing

He's healing the hurts
of this torn and broken heart;
getting me ready
for His progress to start.

The light is now hovering
over dark shadows of my past;
trying to free me
from my torture at last.

The pain is intensified
as it shines on my soul;
I fight and I struggle
as He pleads for control.

Oh! Father, not this one,
I cry and I pray;
the hurt's much too deep,
make the pain go away!

Hush child so gently,
my mind hears Him say;
the pain is for good,
to help the hurt go away …

So I shall surrender
my will now for His;
knowing the *light*
is where my healing is …

It's Only the Beginning

A nine-year vision
has come to pass
God's divine will
unfolding at last

Hold on my child
I'd hear Him say
Do not give up
and do not sway

To the left
nor to the right
Just keep your eyes
fixed on my light

The things I've promised
I'll bring to pass
If you'll just pray
and always ask

So we did
as He commanded
And now look here
where we are standing

It is a dream
we've all prayed for
Not only me
but hundreds more

We're all one body
with only one goal
To bring in the lost
so He can save their soul

We're in the beginning
of our victory won
Standing in the door
of only PHASE ONE!

The road ahead
it's long that's true
But together we'll serve
yes, me and you

For we are the body
and He's the head
We all fit together
as our Father has said

So let us rejoice
in what He has done
And ban together
until the setting sun

For we all know, unless He builds the house
our labor will be in vain
But we're here today, because we dared to believe
In the power of JESUS' name …

It's True! I'm Forgiven!

Father, your forgiveness
is flowing so free;
I accept it now,
in my heart from Thee.

I walked in rebellion,
was disobedient to You;
Now I'm forgiven,
your love is shining through.

Help me to not,
always want my way,
but to know You're supreme;
You know my need for the day.

Teach me, Father,
to be as forgiving as you;
Long-suffering and kind,
extra gentle too.

Let me put,
on the garment of praise;
Whenever I'm burdened,
and my mind's in a daze.

Remind me of songs,
once sang unto You
And how they lift me;
makes my spirit renewed.

This then I can handle
this world with its snares;
Just knowing that YOU,
my God, really cares.

Jesus Cares!

As you walk
through these doors, my friend;
release your burdens
that you hide within.

Know that Jesus,
He cares for you,
wants to heal your heart,
and make it brand-new.

He seeks to save
and bring home the lost;
He shed His blood
to pay the cost.

So if you'll surrender
as you walk through these doors,
you won't leave
as you were before.

He'll take your burdens,
restore your youth;
Because JESUS IS THE WAY,
THE LIFE, AND THE TRUTH!

Jesus Loves Me!

When the trials seem so heavy
   and the burdens I can hardly stand;
I do as God commanded,
   I reach out for His strong hand.

He's never let me down thus far,
   He wouldn't start now I know;
He's been so faithful through the years,
   it's in His word I've grown.

When the waves have tossed me,
   and the waters have seemed so deep—
To Him I turn and cry out,
   and bow before His knee.

He seems to get such pleasure,
   when praises to Him I sing,
and all my burdens are lifted,
   as I stand humbly before my King.

His love He gives so freely,
   during the times that we have shared—
I wonder why I wait so long,
   to bow before Him in prayer!

So when your trials get heavy,
   and your burdens you can hardly stand—
Just go to God in prayer, my friend,
   He's waiting with an outreached hand …

Just Say Thank You

A Thankful heart brings healing.
   A Thankful heart brings Joy …
A Thankful heart brings singing,
   Happiness and so much more …

When clouds roll in and try to hide
   The one you've come to love.
Lift up a Thankful heart my friend.
   Blessings will flow from above …

He loves to bask within our love.
   He loves to hear our Praise.
I sit in awe of our great King.
   Who loves us every day …

Written June 25, 2004

Keeping My Eyes on You

I want to lay aside this world
   its thinking and desires.
I want to hide myself in you,
   and bask in your presence for hours.

The worldly snares come swiftly, Lord,
   like a storm comes upon the sea.
They get me off the course you've set—
   and take my eyes off Thee.

They come in little packages
   all wrapped so pretty and neat.
Disguised with pleasure, marked with sin—
   I know its pain I'll reap.

I need to put my glasses on—
   the spiritual ones You give;
That I may see the wickedness,
   within this world I live.

So I can sail the sea of life,
   directed by your hand.
Setting my eyes upon the goal—
   Your perfect will and plan ...

Ladies Camp Retreat

There is a very special day,
    I wait for every year.
It's called our Ladies Camp Retreat
    and it's coming very near.

The refreshing received
    within our soul,
Could never be bought
    with any man's gold.

Cabins filled with
    fellowship so sweet;
And each of us ladies
    bring a special treat.

Our meals are prepared
    with love and care.
We all do our part
    in the work we share.

This year we'll have a prayer walk;
    what fun that's going to be.
Out praying in the mountain air,
    just Jesus, you, and me.

The classes that we all attend,
    will be of great reward;
Some focus on our Character,
    others on our precious Lord.

Our speaker comes
   with warm-hearted love;
And a message felt
   from God above.

We'll gather in His name up there,
   pray, have fun, and sing.
Altogether in one accord,
   we'll praise our Heavenly King!

So what I'm saying to you today,
   is will you pray and seek?
To see if you can be with us,
   at our ladies camp retreat …

Led to Fast

As I started my day
   I was led to fast.
Not knowing why
   I did not ask.

An experience so new
   this inner voice—
I began to Praise,
   give Thanks, Rejoice!

I went to Church
   the normal time
hung to each word,
   they were just mine.

They were talking of
   a greater power,
that God would give
   this very hour.

A power that comes
   from God alone,
A Comforter—
   to lead me home.

A Baptism not
   from man's own hand,
given to me
   by God's command.

It is a gift
   given to the Saints.
To help them fight
   so they won't faint;

As they fight,
   the "Spiritual Fight,"
inner the darkness,
   take hold of the night.

I took the Scriptures,
   the foundation they laid,
into my room,
   I studied and prayed.

Then I knew
   why I was led to fast,
a preparation time
   for me to ask.

That night I answered
   the altar call.
I needed this gift,
   I needed it all.

I needed "His Strength"
   to be His Soldier in Fight
Oh! How I'm thankful,
   For that precious night …

Let My Voice Ring Loud

Lord here I am again, an empty vessel,
   needing the touch from Your hand.
Drowning in the quicksand of life,
   needing a new look into Your light.

Shine on the depths of my soul. I feel lost and oh, so cold.
   Please Father, don't let go of me, take my hand—
draw me to Your knee
   Where I can sit and feel Your love for me.

My need for You
   is so great, dear Lord—
I'm lonely, sad,
   tattered, and torn.

I feel like a child out of touch
   with its Mother.
With her nurturing love
   that matches no other.

Please, Father, hear my prayer today.
   Please, my Father, before it's too late.
I want nothing in this world, but You—
   let the light of Your love come shining through.

Cast out shadows of darkness in my heart.
   Beam in Your light and give me a new start.
The warm tears on my cheeks are only for You.
   A heart crying out, desperate for truth.

The truth only You my God can fulfill,
  right now as I'm waiting and standing still.
Arms stretched out, toward heaven to You—
  I'm here waiting for the answer to come through.

Have I still got a place in Your heart?
  Please don't tell me I've drifted too far.
I need You and I love You, my precious Lord.
  I'm standing and knocking at heaven's door.

I'm Your child, Lord, and I need You to hear—
  Let my voice ring out loud in Your ear.
I'm Your child, Lord, and I need You to hear—
  Please let my voice, ring loud in Your ear.

I'm Your child, Lord, and I need You to hear …

Written June 10, 1998

Let Us Love You

We've come here today, Lord, to see You.
One glimpse of Your face, brings us peace.
One touch from Your Spirit, brings healing,
as our tears spring forth like rain—bringing release.

We've come here today, Lord, just to love You.
How can we minister to You?
Now, Lord, we open our heart's door,
receive now our love, pouring through.

Receive all our praises, as upward,
Our hearts cry to you, in one accord—
For You alone, Lord, are worthy,
so righteous and Holy, and adored.

We've come here today, Lord, to "love You"—
How can we minister to You?
We've come here today, Lord, to "love You,"
Open Your arms, as our love comes pouring through ...

Letter to a Lonely Heart

Dear lonely heart,
   I know how you feel.
Dear lonely heart,
   I know your pain is real.

I have felt your confusion,
   the overwhelming grief—
Praying each morning,
   would bring me relief.

I have felt the anguish,
   flood over my soul.
To the point that I questioned—
   "God who's in control?"

I felt such darkness,
   till it chilled me to the spine.
At times I even wondered—
   "Was I losing my mind?"

I wanted to run,
   I wanted to hide.
I even felt possibly—
   I wanted to die!

I felt so defeated,
   for in the past I was strong.
Every waking moment—
   I would cry out "What's wrong?"

I felt so alone,
   not a friend could I find—
Then Jesus would whisper,
   "My child, you are mine!"

"You must go through,
   this pain for a while—
Then I will replace
   your tears with a smile."

"For if you cannot feel,
   what another, may feel—
How can you know,
   that their pain is for real?"

I wish I could say,
   I knew all this then;
But Dear Lonely Heart,
   that's where our faith must begin.

We must know that our Father,
   is the potter—we are the clay.
And allow Him to mold us
   and make us what He may.

That He be Glorified,
   through the trials that we face.
Knowing that our strength—
   He will always replace …

Lifeline*

My lifeline cometh
when Your strength flows through my veins
as always it does
when cometh the rains.

My lifeline cometh
straight from Your throne
as You reach down and tell me
I am Your own.

My lifeline cometh
as You show me You care
by placing Your angels
about me, everywhere.

My lifeline cometh
when I hear Your voice
"Arise, my child,
It's time to rejoice!"

---

*   Titled by family

Longing for Jesus

Lord, I don't belong
   on this earth that I trod—
I long to be with you
   on heavenly sod.

I long to sing
   what the angels sing—
I long to worship
   at your feet my King.

I long to gaze
   into your lovely face
and thank You for
   Your "Saving Grace."

I long to sit
   for hours on end—
sharing your fellowship,
   "My Lord, My Friend."

Looking Ahead

Look high upon the mountains,
   soon the flowers will bloom;
To show off God's beauty,
   like the butterfly in the cocoon.

Admire now the loveliness,
   of the trees standing tall;
Just starting to bud,
   putting behind them the fall.

Listen to the birds,
   with their gay melody;
Giving praises of song,
   as to the King of Kings.

Stop for a moment,
   feel the breeze in the air?
The sweet smell of spring,
   blowing through your hair.

Enjoy every second,
   of this God given time;
Stop, look, and listen,
   reaching forward, not behind.

Lost at Sea

There's a lonely tug
　　in my heart tonight.
I'm missing your closeness—
　　I need to draw to the light.

I'm missing the warmth
　　I receive from you,
When I'm down on my knees—
　　troubled and blue.

I'm missing your presence,
　　oh Lord, it's been too long.
My days have been too busy—
　　bring me back where I belong.

When our fellowship is broken
　　and I'm not close by your side,
I feel like I'm drifting
　　out to sea with the tide.

I feel like I'm sailing,
　　cold waters all alone;
With darkness all around me—
　　as I get farther from home.

I feel like I'm caught
　　in the current of life,
Slowly going under—
　　with each breath as I fight.

Now this empty vessel
   is reaching to you,
I feel the gentle waves—
   of your love soaking through.

I feel the sunshine,
   breaking through the dark clouds—
I hear your voice
   speaking so loud;

"I've missed you too
   my precious little one,
Come rest in my arms—
   a new day has begun ..."

Love Gently Blooms

Like a rosebud in bloom,
as it gently unfolds;
I've watched the Lord
bring love to your souls.

I've watched as you two
have walked, hand in hand—
smiling and talking
and making your plans.

The rose petals unfolding
as your love starts to grow—
your caring and sharing
has brought your face a new glow.

He's taken the years
of the sad lonely heart,
replaced it with joy—
as He gives you a new start.

The years of your friendship,
now take a new path—
as God's perfect plan,
has unfolded at last.

I know if my mother
could look down from above,
she'd give you her "blessings"
and send you her "love."

And I know that our God
is with you today—
to honor and bless
your "Wedding Day" …

Written for her dad and his new wife on their wedding day

Love Letter to God

Father, have I told You lately,
　　just how much I care?
Please accept my "thank You"
　　for always being there.

Have I told You that You are,
　　my closest, very best friend?
Your love for me is breathless,
　　there's no beginning—no end.

Have I said, "I love You"
　　other than in a prayer?
Let me tell it to You now,
　　as we share this ocean air.

I love Your created beauty,
　　the mountains stretching high—
The vastness of the ocean,
　　the blue-tint crystal sky.

The water's cleansing power,
　　as the sound rushes through my soul—
I feel so clean and fresh my God,
　　as the waves break forth and roll.

I love Your gentle Spirit,
　　He guides me every day.
He comforts me in sadness,
　　He takes my pain away.

He tells me all about You,
    He helps me know You more.
He teaches me to Honor You,
    as Father and as Lord.

He gives me strength when I am weak,
    He helps me battle the night.
He gives me power through Your word,
    to fight this spiritual fight.

I Love You both, dear Father, God,
    the two of You are one—
You sent Him to me on this earth,
    after You took Your Son.

And speaking of Your Son,
    now, Lord, I love Him most of all—
'Cause He saved me from death and hell,
    my ransom from the fall.

Jesus, my sweet Jesus,
    you bled and died for me—
You took my place upon the tree,
    when You died on Calvary.

Oh! but the story's not ended,
    for the victory was Your own—
You have a place with the Father,
    sitting on the right of His throne.

I love You, Father, Spirit, and Son,
    for the three of You are one—
I'll see You face to face someday,
    when my work on earth is done …

Love Never Fades

I'll never forget my mother, Lord,
    I can still visualize her face.
I know when she laid so sick in bed,
    she was covered with your saving grace.

I remember the glow upon her face,
as she held my hand so tight;
She was walking through the dark with you,
when she told me of the "cross" that night.

She was passing through the valley of death,
    with no fear inside of her heart.
She had that sweet assurance from you,
    that you would never depart.

The things we shared so lovingly,
    as close beside her I stayed;
Will always be a momentum for me,
    until I see her someday.

When You will come for all of us,
    and the clouds will rip asunder;
The dead in Christ shall rise up first,
    'tis then I will see my mother!

Love Ran Deep

And inspirational thought while reading Matthew 26:57–68

Your love sure ran deep,
on that darkened day,
when they rent your clothes,
and pushed you away.

Though they spit on your face,
smote You with their hands,
your love still ran deep,
to follow out God's plan.

How would I have reacted,
my precious Lord,
had I been in your place,
when pushed to the floor?

I know that my love,
could not go that deep,
in my human instinct,
I'd have jumped to my feet.

Ready to defend my honor,
I'm sure—
Wanting them to know,
I was holy and pure.

I'm beginning to see, Lord,
it just had to be—
Only You could face,
the battle for me.

The shedding of your blood,
on Calvary's tree,
was the complete payment,
for a sinner like me …

Love? What Does it Really Mean?

Our world is filled with a great word called "Love,"
  but what does it really mean?
Should we be nice to only those we like?
  That won't change the world that I've seen.

What about those who don't quite agree,
  with everything we may believe.
Do we turn them away, with a grin on our face,
  saying "You haven't seen the light that I've seen."

Sometimes we think we're the only one,
  that holds the key to God's heart.
Somehow I believe from the word that I read—
  His Son died to give all a new start.

There's broken hearts
  in our world out there.
They need to know
  we love them and care.

No matter what
  the barriers may be,
in God's great love—
  there is liberty.

We cannot love
  only those we like,
who suit our fancy—
  and talk just right.

We need to flow
  with compassionate love.
This will give us new insight,
  of our Father above.

His love was so perfect,
  not a respecter of men.
He died for the world,
  to bring us all home again.

So let's not just love,
  only those we like,
who suit our fancy—
  and talk just right.

Let's be like Christ
  and glow with His light—
Whether they be wrong,
  or possibly right.

For of all the gifts which our Father gives,
  the gift of "His Love" is best.
If we will extend our hand out in love—
  our reward will be perfect rest.

So let's put aside our self-righteous love,
  that loves only those we like;
Take up our cross to walk in His path—
  knowing we're doing what's right.

Now let's make a vow to overflow with this love,
  that God gives to us so free;
And let it rise from deep in our hearts—
  to start here with you and with me …

Lover of My Soul

I've never had a lover like You.
  Never had someone love me like You do ...
Never knew someone who could take away my shame ...
  Never knew someone I worshipped as I spoke their name ...

Never knew someone who could bring me to my knees ...
  Or put my feet to dancing as You do my King ...
Never knew someone who could heal my broken heart.
  Never knew someone who would never ever part.

Never knew someone who could show me things to come ...
  Only You, my Jesus, You're the only one ...
Never knew someone the way I know You ...
  Never knew someone who'd do the things that You do ...

You love me like no other could do,
  You take away my shame as I praise and worship You ...
You bring me Joy as I dance before You ...
  You love me Jesus, yes You do ... You love
me Jesus ... I LOVE YOU TOO ...
I count my blessings more and more ...
  I'm so thankful You knocked on my door ...
I'm so thankful I let You in.
  I'm so thankful You are my friend.

Yes, I'm so thankful, my precious Lord.
  Thank You for knocking on my heart's door.
Thank You for being the "Lover of my Soul."
  I praise You now and forever more ...

Written May 27, 2004

Make Me a Blessing

Lord, I want to be a Blessing.
  Let Your light come shining through.
I want others to feel the love,
  that comes only from knowing You.

Make me a Blessing when I open my mouth.
  Guard my lips, that I do not bring—
Reproach upon Your lovely name,
  my Father, King of Kings.

Let my hands always be ready
  and my arms wide open too—
For those who need forgiveness—
  The love is found in You.

Let my eyes show mercy
  to those I look upon,
and may I never, ever judge—
  so their faith will linger on.

Let my feet be swift to walk,
  in places far and near;
As the Spirit guides me—
  and whispers in my ear.

Set a watch upon my heart,
  let no bitterness or strife;
Be allowed to fester there—
  For Jesus You Are My Life!

Inspired by my friend Nora

You are a Blessing to me.
Thank you for sharing His love with me.

Freda

Mary Did Your Heart Break?

Oh precious Mary, how your heart must have broken—
    As you watched your son, hang in the air ...
Cold and lifeless, between two thieves—
    You watched Him dying there.

As you sat nursing Him as a little babe,
    Cuddled in your arms so tight ...
Did you ever for a moment have any indication—
    Of what He would face that night?

Did you ever lay awake late at night,
    As you listened to His every breath—
Think for one moment in the quietness of night—
    That you would watch Him struggle with death?

I'm sure He brought you many hours of joy,
    As you watched Him grow into a man ...
Strong in spirit, mighty in strength—
    He followed out the Father's plan.

I'm sure you knew from the very beginning,
    You had a very special child ...
I know the Father covered you with grace,
    As He walked with you—down, that dreaded mile ...

I'm thankful you raised Him as the Father told you to ...
    He taught in the synagogues—He preached to the crowds ...
He's one in the Spirit—He's the Father, He's the Son ...
    We'll all see Him one day—when He bursts through the clouds!

Written May 29, 2002

Memory Book

Women keep a "Memory Book" …
   It's called …"Those who've touched my heart" …
I've placed you on the first page, my friend …
   Because I've loved you from the start …

As I look upon your life …
   Your sweet and gentle ways …
I know you keep my Jesus …
   First on your list each day …

I know that He has been the one …
   Who has made you who you are …
He's given you so many gifts …
   The biggest is … your "Tender Heart" …

As a little girl I know …
   You used to dream of "love" …
You asked the Lord to "Bless" your life …
   So came Brother Hart…on the wings of a "Dove" …

The two of you have been through much …
   Fifty years is a very long time …
But oh! the joys you've shared together …
   So precious in your mind …

So many times I know you've prayed …
   For others throughout the years …
You've brought them to … the "Throne Room of God" …
   With a humble heart and tears …

Someday you'll see the benefits ...
   Of all that you have done ...
When Jesus runs into your arms ...
   And says ... "Well done, my Precious one!" ...

Written April 27, 2000

Merry Christmas, Daddy

Merry Christmas, Daddy,
   you've been on my heart so strong;
Even though I miss you,
   you're right where you belong …

Memories of you—of times we shared,
   coming flooding through my mind …
Bringing me hope, peace, and joy—
   as I reflect on each special time …

Each Christmas now will be different,
   a chapter in my life is through.
I want to thank you, Daddy,
   for the fun times I had with you …

The fishing trips of course were the best.
   picnics at the Beach were too …
Sidewalk skates at Christmas time,
   were my favorite gifts from you …

As each one holds a warm memory,
   I'm tucking them deep in my heart;
Reminding me of the love we shared,
   though for a time we are apart …

I'm looking forward, Daddy,
   to that time we again will meet;
When heaven becomes a reality—
   when we're worshipping at Jesus's feet …

Just one more thing please, Daddy,
    will you give Him a hug for me?
Wish Him happy birthday—
    sing it to our Lord and King ...

Merry Christmas, Daddy
Happy Birthday, Jesus ...

I love You, Freda

Written December 24, 2003

Morning Hideaway

There is a place I need to go
as my feet step out of bed.
To fall down on my knees to You,
and lift my heart and head.

As I call upon Your name
giving honor to only You—
You will give the strength I need,
You'll guide me all day through.

For when I do not seek your face,
first thing when out of bed,
I find my path has gone astray—
myself has only led.

So open my eyes, dear God, today,
to put my priorities straight.
To sit before your presence, Lord—
and enter Your *Holy Gate* ...

Mother

M   Is for my *Mother*, whom I love so very dear.
O   Is for *Obedience* she teaches to me still.
T   Is for the *Tender Tears* she cries upon her bed.
H   Is for the *Halo* that I see upon her head.
E   Is for *Eternally* grateful that I am.
R   Is for *Remembrance* of her I'll always have.

Now put them all together, and as you all can see that they spell my
MOTHER
She means the world to me.

Written May 1982

Mother's Day*

You're so much like
A mother to me
I could not pass
The opportunity
To show you my love
That's straight from the heart
It's been there for you
Right from the start
You've brought new hope
And love to my life
And helped me remove
Great bitterness and strife
So now my prayer
Is coming your way
"Dear Father, bless her
On this Mother's Day!"

---

* Titled by family

Moving Away[*]

You've meant so many things to me
To list just one, would be a waste
I guess the thing I love the most
Is the glow I see upon your face.
What will I do without your smile
Your encouraging words unending
I guess like you, I'll have to start
A life of new beginnings
The priceless times that we have shared
The movies we have seen
Will be to me a treasure
Tucked deep inside my heart
I know that God has given us
A "special friendship" touch
And He will be our bond
Because we love Him so much
He will supply for you and me
As days and years go by
As He has done so many times
On this we can rely
And so the time has come my friend
That we must say goodbye
But only for a while, you see
'Cause I'll be back from time to time!

Written to a friend during the time our family
was relocating from Utah to Washington

---

[*] Titled by Family

My Best Friend

I sat down tonight
   and shed a tear …
I was thinking of our friendship—
   throughout this past year …

So many times,
   you've brought joy to me …
My heart has laughed,
   through tears of glee …

When times I've been sad,
   you are always there—
Your encouraging words
   make my sorrows easier to bear …

The warmth and love
   you've extended to me—
Is a precious gift of God—
   and I thank Him daily …

When the sun shines on my day,
   making the skies a crystal blue—
I can't help thinking,
   of my love for you …

A friend is a treasure
   far greater than pearls—
And you are the "Best Friend"—
   in the whole wide world …

Written April 4, 2001

My Brother, My Friend

Well, here we are again, Lord,
    another life has come to an end …
I not only called him "Brother," Lord,
    because Timmy was my friend …

We know he wasn't perfect, Lord,
    none of us can be …
I loved his boyish nature,
    that made Timmy special to me …

If I were to close my eyes right now,
    I could see his teasing grin …
I knew he was up to something,
    my silly little friend …

I use to hold my breath at times,
    when I'd see that smile on his face …
I wondered if he had planted some fireworks,
    in a strange unusual place …

He was a jokester,
    this brother of mine,
from the beginning of childhood,
    till the end of his time …

I wouldn't have had it
    any other way
'cause Timmy brought laughter
    to others' each day …

I thank You, Lord,
   for the years with him—
and as You hold him
   could You tell my friend—

That he was special
   in so many ways,
and I'll be there with him
   again someday …

Inspirational by
Freda Westnedge
Written for Timmy on Wednesday August 29, 2001

    Mom wrote this poem for her brother, Timmy, and she read it at his funeral. She loved him very much.

In loving memory of Timmy
May 1963–August 2001

My Cyber Friend

I sit here and laugh
At the things that you say
You bring smiles to my face
And you brighten my day

I thank the Lord
For allowing us to meet
Your friendship is a blessing
And I think you're so sweet

It amazes me still
How He brings hearts together
I pray we will always
Be friends forever

I love You
Have a blessed day
P.S. Thanks for inspiring this little poem. Written just for you!

Freda Westnedge
April 28, 2000

My Dad

I know I haven't told you lately,
　　just how I really feel.
I want you now to know, my dad;
　　my love for you is real.

I've gone too long with words untold,
　　the time has now arrived;
to open up my heart to you,
　　and say what's deep inside.

Did you think I did not know,
　　the many times you cried,
wanting me to feel your love,
　　yet thought you had to hide.

Did you think I did not see
　　the hurt within your heart?
when you had to punish me,
　　hoping my love would not depart.

Did you think I did not see
　　all the worried looks,
when I laid so sick in bed;
　　the turns you and mom took?

Did you think I did not see,
　　the sacrifices made,
for me to have the nicest things
　　within your limited pay?

Did you think I did not hear
   the discussions for my good?
although you felt I did not care,
   I really understood.

I've seen your precious guiding hand,
   throughout the years, my dad;
and want you now to know for sure,
   your daughter's very glad;

To have a dad so wonderful,
   as you have been to me;
in such a blessing to my heart,
   I pray that you can see.

I hope that we can be good friends,
   and always keep in touch;
because my very SPECIAL DAD,
   I Love You Very Much!

My Dad Is Home

It doesn't take much for me to remember my Dad ...
    All I have to do is close my eyes, and his face is before me ...
Think of his love
    and he's right there in my heart ...

Just thinking of all the wonderful things he did for me,
    brings memories flooding in like waves
beating against the rocks ...
I can see him now in my mind's eye, walking on streets of gold ...
    Singing in the "Son" shine ... Well, happy, and whole!

My Love for You

Although I've never seen your face—
    Or been able to give you a hug …
My heart's connected to you, my friend,
    From my Father up above …

I may not be the best at words,
    My talents are very few—
Yet, I will always extend my hand
    In friendship unto you …

Our skin may be a different shade,
    Our speech may be different too—
Our homes are many miles apart,
    Yet I have this love for you …

I know someday I'll meet you friend—
    Just when I do not know …
You'll know me by the glow on my face—
    And the witness in my soul …

You see it's God that connects our hearts—
    His love is in the air …
I do not need to see your face,
    To know how much you care …

I feel it in the words you type,
    I hear it in your voice …
Your love for Him comes shining through—
    In Him we both rejoice!

I do not understand it all—
    How we're connected here on earth …
I know it's from our Father's love—
    I know it's from *Rebirth*!

It's born of the *Spirit*, of *Water*, and of *Blood*—
    It's born of the sacrifice …
It's born in the *Kingdom, Heaven's own Throne*—
    Because He paid the price …

I LOVE YOU, MY CYBERFRIEND … I'LL SEE YOU IN
HEAVEN, IF NOT ON THIS EARTH BELOW …
Written May 28, 2002

My Love Is Still Here

It's been many years now …
　Since my precious mother, was called away …
But the love inside my heart and the memories in my mind …
　Will always be there to stay …

All I have to do to feel her love …
　Is close my eyes … and reminisce …
Her beautiful face … and lovely smile …
　Brings "joy" in moments like this …

I can almost feel her loving arms …
　As so gently we both embrace …
As I tell her that the years gone by …
　Have not made my love erase …

I want so much within my heart, to honor her …
　On this "special" day …
As I did, many times before …
　By things I would do and say …

She did not have the wealth of many …
　But she was rich beyond compare …
She had the priceless love of Jesus …
　And she shared it everywhere …

She did not have to speak a word …
　You could see it in her eyes …
You could feel it in her handshake …
　As she touched you when you walked by …

She loved the simple things in life …
   Like squirrels running in the yard at play …
A fresh falling snow in wintertime …
   To her … was a "perfect" day …

Her flowers brought many hours of joy …
   She loved the beauty that they shared …
Many times a bouquet she'd pick …
   To tell someone that she cared …

She loved to take a special piece …
   Of fabric in her hand …
And she would make a pattern …
   Without a written plan …

She shared her love for sewing …
   With children everywhere …
Through blankets … special clothing …
   Or a big soft "teddy bear" …

She loved to listen to "country gospel" …
   She swayed to the music and clapped her hands …
She had a radiant glow on her face …
   As they sang of "Heaven" and "Bulah" land …

I think she always knew somehow …
Her time on earth was short …
Maybe that's why she loved so deeply …
Before she had to report …

I often wonder how she's doing …
   In "Heaven," so far away …
I long to give her a "great big hug" …
   And wish her "Happy Mother's Day" …

But since I can't … I'll ask you, Lord …
    Give her my "love" I pray …
Hold her tight in your arms for me …
    Till I meet her again someday …

Written May 9, 2000

My Mother, My Friend

Next to You, Lord, I lost my best friend today.
  The pain is extremely deep.
Without You in my heart, Jesus,
  I know I could not sleep.

What will tomorrow bring for me?
  Will I be able to laugh and smile?
Please hold me in your arms real tight,
  let's just sit here for a while.

I know she's very happy, Lord,
  up there in your presence now;
Surely these tears won't last forever,
  I'll make it through somehow.

I praise You through these tears, Lord,
  for giving her to me;
Our relationship was so "special,"
  because of her love for Thee.

She taught me what true love was,
  not to look on the outside of me;
But to put my trust and life in your hands,
  only then would I be able to see.

She lived her life before me, an example;
  clean, pure, kind, and good.
I want to follow in her footsteps,
  with your help I know I could.

So now as Your strength flows throughout my veins,
    I'll hold my head up high;
Looking forward to that wonderful day,
    we'll have our reunion in the sky …

Inspirational by
Freda Westnedge

Mom wrote this poem a long time ago to her mother who passed away in 1981. We loved this poem, and we put it on Mom's Celebration of Life flyer as well as on bookmarks with her picture given to family and friends.

We'll never forget you, MOM! WE LOVE YOU!

In loving memory of Freda Westnedge
May 1946–February 2017

My Spirit Soars

My spirit soars
   in praise to my King.
My Father, my God,
   my everything.

As words spring forth
   may they honor only you.
Nothing in this world
   brings joy like You do.

Nothing can make
   this heart feel at peace
other than You, Jesus;
   It's your presence I seek.

I feel the warmth
   of your spirit in me.
I rise to give honor
   and praises to Thee.

I hear your whispers
   of wisdom, of truth.
My heart is light,
   my spirit renewed.

You have held me forever within your love.
   My hand you have never let go.
As father and daughter we walk side by side,
   your faithfulness is what I know …

In the highest of mountains,
    in the beauty of the sea.
In gardens of flowers,
    your love comes to me.

You painted this picture
    for my eyes to behold.
In the beauty of this tapestry,
    your love is told.

Written February 16, 2005

No Number Needed

Don't bother taking a number,
'cause God will hear you now.
Just open up your heart my friend,
and speak to Him out loud.

He's listening ever so closely,
to what you have to say;
He watches over you each night—
He guides you through your day.

He wants to know what's on your heart,
your burdens He will bear.
He's saying now to you, my friend—
"Come talk to me in prayer."

No One Can Know

No one can know
how lonely you feel,
and no one can really know,
the pain though its real.
The heartache you feel inside
is so intensified—
no one can know, no one can know.

No one can know
the road you've been down,
the many times, you surely thought,
you'd fall to the ground.
Temptations that come your way,
you fight day by day—
no one can know, no one can know.

No one can know
how you've cried out for help,
and thought that no one cared,
and life was unfair—
So many times the bitterness,
has welled up inside—
no one can know, no one can know.

But I have a friend
who knows every heart,
the loneliness that you feel,
through Him will depart.
He's already paid the price—
on Calvary's tree,
Yes I have a friend, He'll be your friend.

So now take, that step of faith
and reach out to Him,
you'll find that He's always cared—
and He'll be your friend.
He'll lead you and guide you, each step of the way,
you'll have a friend, a friend till the end,
He'll be your friend.

So now take, that step of faith
and reach out to Him.
You'll have a friend, a friend till the end,
He'll be your friend …

And that friend is Jesus …

Originally written by Freda as a Song

No Record in Heaven

I'm glad You keep no record, Lord,
　　of the wrong things I do and say.
I'm glad You have a bending heart,
　　when I don't do things your way.

Oh! how many times I must have hurt you,
　　by all I say and do.
Please, my Father, teach me,
　　to be still and trust in you.

Help me see your guiding hand,
　　in all my cherished thoughts.
That I may cling to those so pure,
　　and dismiss the ones which are not.

Help me keep my mouth from sin,
　　that I may someday be.
A strong victorious Christian,
　　with your love shining out from me ...

Nursery

My Mother's Jewel,
 that's what I am.
She loves me so I'm told,
 and when she places me in here,
it's for my good I know.

She cares for me so very much,
 that's why she won't return.
To see if I am satisfied,
 because I'll fret and churn.

I'll try to be so very good,
 peaceful, sweet, and kind.
'Cause God loves order in his church,
 I'll try my best to mind.

Visiting is not allowed,
 I cannot talk to you.
Once my mommie puts me here,
 I'll stay until she's through.

The ladies are so very sweet,
 they give to me their time.
I'll be as patient as can be,
 and wait my turn in line.

They are so very qualified,
 and take good care of me.
Just drop me at the door today,
 and all your fears will leave ...

Written by request for the nursery

247

O Death Where Is Thy Sting

Death is all around us here,
we see it everywhere.
Yet our Savior says to us,
"Lo, I'll be with you there."

The parting is not easy,
of loved ones so dear and kind;
but we know not the wise ways of God,
His mighty thoughts or His mind.

We know His word is true today,
"All things work together for our good,"
although our minds reach out and say,
"Why? And are you sure it could?"

It is not wrong to ask of Him,
"Please, Father, reveal your plan,"
help me see your precious love,
to know it's You in command.

Help me through my tears, dear Lord,
to praise your holy name—
to know You are forever,
yesterday, today, the same.

Keep me in Your loving arms,
as onwardly we press—
Help me give You every care,
my burdens, and my stress.

For now we see only partly,
through the glass so dim and gray—
We know within our hearts, dear God,
Your plan is the perfect way.

We know You cannot lie, dear Lord,
You love us oh so much—
our sorrows, griefs, infirmities,
You feel the very touch.

So guard me through the storms ahead,
as a mother bird does her nest—
Give me now, my Father above,
Your lasting peaceful rest ...

One Day[*]

The sun was shining brightly
Children were happily at play
I went about my duties
In the normal everyday way

My home was warm and cozy
My family, fed and clothed
We had a lot of material gain
So happy in our little abode

Yet something deep inside was aching
Dissatisfaction was creeping in
Darkness overshadowed
Within my heart this darkness lived

Then a loved one entered the scene
With a gift, it seemed for me
He had no price upon his gift
For me he said it was free

The gift he offered was freedom
From the darkness that was covering me
He said it came from Jesus
To be kept for Eternity

I had a choice to make that day
Accept the freedom plea
Or stay locked up inside my walls
The dark that was tormenting me

---

[*] Titled by family

I reached out quickly and took the gift
I held it to my heart
I thanked my Jesus for saving me
And repented in my heart

Only a Moment

Times like these are very hard,
    on family and on friends.
A loved ones past beyond the gates—
    "Eternal life to live."

Memories flood, flashing through our minds,
    of moments throughout the years.
Some bring joy, contentment, and peace,
    others bring only tears.

Some bring thoughts of dreams fulfilled,
    others of words untold—
A fleeting wish for one more time,
    your loved one you could hold.

The words you wish you could have said,
    ring loudly within your ear—
But do not sorrow now, my friend,
    your loved one is very near.

Right there within your heart and thoughts,
    the special moments you shared—
A "special talk," a look of love,
    you showed them how you cared.

At times like these we also think,
    of others that we know.
Friendships broken, loved ones hurt,
    maybe from years ago.

It wakes us up to realize,
    life's too precious and too short—
Let us take this day in time,
    mend friendships, help families be restored.

Let us take the time each day,
    to show others that we care;
Knowing that we may not have—
    "A moment here to spare" …

Only One Love

There is only one love that can change the world—
And, Lord, that love comes straight from You.
There's only one love that can make a heart new—
Lord, that love comes straight from You.

There's only one love that can renew my mind—
That love comes only from You.
It can change all my thoughts, give me direction anew.
Lord, that love comes straight from You.

There's only one love that gives me strength to forgive—
That love, Lord, comes straight from You.
Helps me overlook hurts that cut to the heart—
Lord, that love comes only from You.

There's only one love that brings healing to the soul—
Lord, that love comes only from You.
Rips out the old, brings in life brand-new.
Lord, that love comes only from You.

You're the author, the finisher of things great and small.
Your light shines through darkness, breaks down all our walls.
The work that You do is complete in our hearts,
'Cause that love comes only from You.

Please baptize me now, Lord, with your gift of love—
Which flows straight from heaven, from your throne room above.
It removes all my doubts, makes the darkness recede—
Lord, that love is all that I need.

Lord, Your love is all that I need.

Originally written by Freda as a song

Only You

Jesus, how I wish that I
   could take their pain away.
I wish that I could wipe their tears,
   and make it all okay.

But, Jesus, that just cannot be,
   the strength they need is you—
Help me God to give your love,
   I know you'll see them through.

Let me be your instrument
   Lord, molded by your hand,
And through your love and tenderness,
   reach to my fellow man;

Help me know that *"Only You"*
   can open eyes so blind
And soften hearts with years of pain—
   renew their thoughts and mind.

For when our eyes are fixed on you,
   the Spirit will reveal—
The truth that lies within your word,
   He makes it all so real.

And if an error should come from man
   He makes the truth be known.
Gives witness to the heart of man—
   of God upon the throne.

Open the Door

He'll give you blue skies
Where clouds were before
There's so much waiting
If you'll open that door
He'll tell you He loves you
In so many ways
You'll have true happiness
As you go through your day
So if you don't know Him
And feel as I once did
Just open up your heart now
A new life He will give.

Pain So Deep

I run to you with my broken heart,
I lay myself at your feet.
Pain so unbearable it cuts to my soul,
Lord, your servant is in need.

I know you care for me, dear Lord,
as we walk this road of life.
You've been so faithful through the years,
through my valleys, tears, and strife.

As I call upon your name, meditating upon your Word,
I wonder—Lord, what would you do?
Then ever so softly your voice I hear—
"Show my love child, as I've shown to you."

Wounds of enemies, friends or foes,
penetrate to the deepest part of the heart ...
As I stay close to you, with your light shining through,
the healing now begins to start ...

Ministering angels all around me so near,
bringing words of comfort and peace ...
Looking upwards to you, now my strength is renewed—
This pain, Lord, to *You* I release ...

Plow Up My Field, Lord!

When my strength
   seems to fade away;
when I'm weary
   too weak to pray.

I roll my cares
   upon my Lord,
for He has promised
   that He'd restore.

For in my weakness
   He'll make me strong,
to walk in the spirit
   where I belong.

He'll hold my hand
   till I come through,
this one more trial, today,
   that's new;

Each one had purpose
   within my life;
some bring healing
   others strife.

It's up to me,
   now will I yield?
allow Him to dig,
   plow up my field.?

I know His plan
    is to make me whole,
bring in the new
    take out the old;

If I will allow
    His refining fire,
to purify me
    this very hour!

Power of the Spirit

No one can stand under the power of your Spirit, Lord,
And not be touched;
They may reject it, ignore it, not understand it;
But they know they need it very much.

No one can stand under the power of your Spirit, Lord,
And not receive conviction of sin;
They may fight it, and sometimes try to hide it,
Yet know they need a cleansing from within.

No one can stand under the power of your Spirit, Lord,
When your healing touch begins;
They may reject it, pretend it's not effective;
But in the end, you'll win.

No one can stand under the power of your Spirit, Lord,
When the Spirit's moving free;
Walking up and down the aisles, revealing the Son and Thee;
Oh Father, why won't they see!

Why do they stand under the power of your Spirit, Lord?
Rejecting the call within, "Come unto me all ye heavy laden;
Reach out your hand, place it in mine, and I will give you rest,
I'm offering my very best!"

I guess that's why the choices are mine, my Lord,
When I stand under the power of your Spirit;
I open my heart, receive all from You,
By letting your sweet Spirit flow through.

Oh, how I praise your sweet Holy name,
And the Spirit that's flowing through;
I lift up my hands, to receive your great plan,
I connect now my Spirit with You!

Praise Him!

Oh! ring sweet praises, ring loud and clear.
For God is listening with an open ear.

Our praise is the channel into His throne.
He loves the aroma, He's blessed by our song.

He inhabits our praises, let's sing, let's sing,
and fill the heavens for the King of Kings.

Exalt Him, Exalt Him, lift Him high,
let your love reach to the sky.

Bless Him, Bless Him, for He is great!
Ring forth now Praises into His Gates …

Prayer of Love

The Look upon their faces
    were as angels smiling at me.
The sweetness of their spirits,
    brought "*Refreshing Love*" from thee.

I "Thank You" for these souls, dear Lord,
    you've placed within my care—
I want to be your instrument,
    to lift their needs in prayer.

The hunger in their hearts to know
    the best you have for them;
Has brought them here today, dear Lord,
    they want to touch—your "Garment Hem."

I vow to be so faithful, Lord
    in reaching out in love,
For each one is so "special"
    so gentle as a dove.

I vow to keep an open door
    to my home, my heart, my ear—
In case there be a need for them
    to come and shed a tear.

So give me what I need, dear Lord,
    flow through me like a flood—
To minister your word in "Strength"
    and sprinkled by your blood …

Prayer Partners

It's Valentine's Day
   expressions of love.
The greatest to be
   the Father's above.

We've been through a lot
   the three of us.
Sometimes good—
   others rough.

Yet we've known
   right from the start,
we've had a calling
   within our hearts.

To take our loved ones
   to His throne,
Pray protection—
   from things unknown.

It's been a blessing,
   the things we've learned.
We've grown in love,
   through the trust we've earned.

Thank You for
   your FAITHFULNESS,
LOVE, SUPPORT,
   TRUSTWORTHINESS ...

I LOVE YOU!
Freda

Prayers Of the Saints

I think of my Mother,
sweet Jesus, a lot;
And all of the good things,
from her I was taught.

I miss her sweet smile
and long for her touch;
I want to be with her,
I still love her so much.

The home where she lived,
it's not the same anymore;
The laughter and love,
isn't there like before.

The ones left behind
seem so lost in despair;
I remember how often,
she would take them to prayer.

She wanted so much
for them to know of Your love;
And all of the good things,
You would send from above.

She wanted Your peace
to reign in their hearts;
Your strength to be theirs;
Yet they wanted no part.

I remember the nights,
when in her deepest pain;
With no thought of herself,
she'd call out their name.

So now with time past,
I too search the face,
of these precious dear loved ones;
And still there's no trace.

Yet I know it is written,
about the prayers of the saints;
How Jesus is standing,
at their door and He waits.

For just one soft moment,
a cry from the heart;
He's ready to enter,
and He'll do His part.

So Jesus I promise,
I will see her through;
I'll pick up her prayers,
and lift them to You.

'Cause Jesus, I think
of my Mother a lot,
and all of the good things
from her I was taught …

Purity

Change me, Lord
　　that's what I pray;
Cleanse my heart,
　　please start today.

Take from me
　　what I can't see,
that keeps me from
　　your *purity*.

Wash me white,
　　yes, white as snow;
Grant me grace,
　　let no sin grow.

Open my eyes
　　that I may see,
the good in others;
　　let no judgment be.

Take from me
　　the barriers deep,
that build up walls;
　　tear down I plead.

Take this mouth
　　with cutting lips,
pour in your love;
　　give words that lift.

Take from me,
   my prideful heart,
Please, dear Jesus,
   Come do your part.

Take from me,
   what I can't see,
that keeps me from
   your *purity* ...

Putting Away the Doubts

Doubt I, Lord? Like Thomas did?
   I never thought I would.
So many things I don't understand—
   Oh, how I wish I could.

A walk of faith that's what I hear—
   You must walk through the dark.
And from the guided word You gave,
   I must not ever depart.

Lean not unto your own strength child,
   These words I read so clear.
Will I not make a way for you,
   staying so closely near?

I feel You wooing me, dear Lord,
   You're trying to get through;
To lift me up on higher ground—
   Yet I'm afraid of You.

I'm like Thomas when I cannot see,
   What's coming up the road.
Although I know it's best for me,
   I need your hand to hold.

I know it's not really You I doubt,
   it's things around that I see—
What's that You're saying to me, my Lord?
   Ah, yes, keep my eyes fixed only on Thee!

Putting On Christ

I am a sinner, saved only by grace—
    touched by the Master's hand …
No greater goal, for me on earth,
    than to seek my Father's plan …

He created me "special," there's no two alike,
    He breathed life's breath in me …
He guides my path, directs my steps,
    since the day He set me free …

Since I've laid down my life, to walk in His path,
    no greater joy have I known …
I seek His face, for direction each day,
    as I come boldly unto His throne …

Does this mean I won't suffer? I dare say not—
    the pain I take willingly …
He took all my shame, when He died in my place—
    I gladly give all of me …

Written January 28, 2002

Reaching Out

Take my hands, Lord
please let them reach
to hurting souls
that walk the streets.

Baptize me
with love on high
that they may feel
when they walk by.

Let my words
be soft and sweet;
encouraging to
the ones I meet.

Plant your word
deep in my heart;
give me boldness
to do my part.

Let your light
shine in my eyes;
may it draw them
to your side.

May I serve
in good deeds too;
and together we'll bring
them back to you.

Reflections of Love

Think with me for just a moment,
of someone you really love.
Someone who's always on your mind—
Someone you think the whole world of.

Now think of all their attributes,
their personality traits;
A sweet disposition, a heart of gold—
Just everything that makes them great.

Close your eyes and feel their love
it's there, even though you are apart.
Now think of all the special feelings—
that are churning in your heart.

A love so deep
you can't understand;
You want to reach out
And take them by the hand.

A heart of forgiveness,
no matter what they've done—
It may be a father,
A husband, or a son.

Even the bad things,
that's crept in from time to time;
Will not destroy this image
That you have focused in your mind.

This love you feel has depth,
nothing can rip it apart.
They've gone into your soul—
They're rooted in your heart.

Now think with me for just a moment,
about another *Love* …
A *Love* that's far beyond our capacity—
The *Love* of our Father above.

Now think of all His attributes,
His personality traits;
Giving, loving, forgiveness—
Just everything that makes Him great.

Now close your eyes and feel "*His Love*"—
He's here, you're not apart;
If you've asked Him to come in—
He's there, right in your heart!

He promised He'd never go away
or leave you alone to face the day;
He promised He'd love you till the end—
He promised to return and bring you home again.

His *Love* is running ever so deep,
nothing can rip it apart;
He's gone into your soul—
He's rooted in your heart.

Yes, our sin,
creeps in from time to time.
It will not destroy His love—
We are the focus of His mind.

His *Love* is unconditional,
not from any merits we have done.
It has withstood the test of time—
The perfect price paid by His Son ...

So do not doubt "*His Love*" my friend,
even when the feelings are not there.
Just stand upon His word today—
Believe it! He really cares!

Rejoice!

My God, my God, I love You so.
You've given to me, new love untold.

My heart's so full of praise for you;
I cannot sleep, my love is renewed.

You've given new hope, new joy, new peace;
My spirit's so full, my tongue won't cease.

To praise You, God, is my only desire,
with hands raised high and my lips on fire.

Speaking forth your truth into my soul,
that I might feel your love unfold.

My searching now has come to an end;
New life in You will now begin.

The valley was deep You brought me through,
you said, "Hang on, my word is truth.

I'll never leave You, nor go away,
and through tribulations, I'll make a way;

For You to stand and fight for me
planted strong and firm just like a tree.

Yes, my child, you ran the race,
you fought so hard to see my face;

And now you know that love's the key,
so here I am take all of me.

For I am your God, and I love you so,
Now tell my people wherever you go.

I am their God, their very best friend;
I've given my Son to bring them home again.

They must repent and come unto me.
For time is short, my salvation is FREE!"

So harken now! Oh! hear His call
rejoice with me, come one, come all.

Take and drink, His cup is free,
His blood was shed for you and for me ...

Remembering the '50s

Now in the year of the '50s,
was a grand old time to be.
There were some changes up the road,
that would affect you and me.

One very pretty sunny day,
I started out the door;
My mother looked at me so shocked,
she fainted on the floor.

"They're bobby socks," I said to her;
"Aren't they neat and cool?
And when I do the ROCK 'N' ROLL,
the kids will all just drool!"

Now sister liked the Pat Boone style,
but me, I liked my Elvis.
Although my judgment got real weak,
when I'd see him shake his pelvis.

And this one I can tell for sure,
is bound to get her goat;
I wore my two-piece bathing suit—
She made me put on my coat!

Now when my boyfriend Jack,
came by;
My mother looked at him
and sighed …

What's happened to your hair my boy,
you look so very pale?"
He looked at her and smiled real big,
"They call this a ducktail!"

One day my mother
said to me,
"Let's go to town
on a shopping spree."

I followed her
all through the store—
She bought me a poodle skirt;
It nearly touched the floor!

Oh! Mother dear,
why can't you see?
I can't wear that,
it's past my knee!

It's bad enough
to wear saddle shoes,
Oh! Will I survive
these years with you?

So in the year of the '50s,
with the ponytail and more …
They could not match what we have now,
In the year of '84.

Remember the Call

There's times when I
just don't understand.
there's times when I
question Your mighty hand.

There's times when I lay
all broken and torn—
scarred from the battles,
weary from the storm.

There's times when I fail,
I cry all through the night.
Until I realize—
it's Your battle, Your fight ...

There's times when I
feel like giving up—
pleading with You Father,
"Please take this cup."

Then new strength
flows straight from Your throne—
and my eyes again,
are fixed on Home.

A Home that You
are preparing for me—
filled with love,
where I will be free;

Free from my tears,
heartache and pain—
resting in You—
and my eternal gain.

Now these battles—
they all seem so small—
as I once again focus—
on my purpose, my Call ...

Reporting for Orders

A good night's rest
brings new thoughts of your face,
racing to my heart—
I'm ready now to taste;

The goodness of your word,
what will I learn today?
Give me your wisdom—
In your will I long to stay.

Give me instructions
from your word as I read,
help me to know—
What's my job, what's the need?

Help me to walk
in the steps like You walked—
Put encouraging words
in my mouth as I talk.

And tune my ears
to hear the words of your voice—
As I start now my day, Lord,
in "Your Love I Rejoice!"

Rest for the Spirit

Like a mighty Thunder
the waves came rolling in …
Birds were finding breakfast,
out on the sand again …

The wind was briskly blowing.
Clouds were nestled high.
Time had come for us to leave—
It was time to say goodbye …

The tranquility of the ocean,
with its beauty so serene;
Had once again been faithful,
to bring sweet peace to me …

I gaze upon the horizon.
The sun is shining bright.
My spirit's fully rested,
making everything all right …

Written April 14, 2004

Retreat of a Lonely Heart

The ocean was scenic,
   a soft breeze was in the air.
Soon all the women
   in one room would gather there.

Their hearts were expecting,
   their hopes—all lifted high.
They all were anticipating—
   the Holy Spirit to drop by.

Now they were arriving,
   filtering in one by one;
With name tags in hand—
   the weekend had begun.

What was in store,
   for these hungry, thirsty hearts?
Would they be obedient?
   Let God rip them apart?

Would they lay their wounds open
   and say, "Lord here I am,
Mold me and make me,
   line up with your plan."

"Purify my heart,
   rip out what's unclean;
Make me a vessel—
   one that's clean—one with sheen."

Would they be willing
    to die to themselves?
To extend out a hand—
    to a stranger or someone else?

Would they dare to venture
    outside their comfort zone?
Or stay all snuggled up,
    where it was warm and felt like home.

These were the visions and questions,
    racing through my mind;
As I stood there watching,
    waiting my turn in line.

Then it was time,
    the meeting had begun.
The announcements were made,
    the songs had been sung.

Yes, it was happening,
    He was faithful—He had come.
The Precious Holy Spirit—
    was ministering to each one.

There were faces all aglow,
    there were tear-stained cheeks.
Rewards were being paid;
    to the faithful—who had prayed for weeks.

There was praise and much worship,
    our hands were lifted high.
I felt that the Father—
    was pleased with the sight.

There was laughter and fun,
   and friendly smiling faces—
Food, drinks, and
   friendship embraces.

Yet somewhere in the dark,
   hidden corner of a heart—
tears of *loneliness*,
   was ripping it apart.

Someone was hurting,
   my heart was going out—
To that precious voice,
   it was crying oh so loud.

And since I too,
   have experience with that pain—
I began to weep,
   my composure I could not regain.

And yet down the hall,
   rang laughter, with tears of joy—
Acceptance and friendship,
   was there behind the door.

Yet that lonely heart
   felt cold and all alone.
Having no friendship—
   that she could call her own.

Yes, His sweet Spirit
   was filtering the air.
The choice now was ours—
   to release it—to share;

To throw open our doors,
  extend our hands out in love—
Die to ourselves—
  be gentle as a dove.

Oh, precious saints,
  we must walk as did He;
Extending our hands to the lonely—
  to those in need.

Let us not close
  our hearts to their cries;
But pray to the Father—
  to open our eyes ...

Received April 16, 1996, 8:05 a.m.

Riches Untold

His blessings are not
just silver and gold;
as a matter of fact
they are riches untold.

Like the smile of a child,
the twinkle in their eye
when you give them a kiss,
or sing them a lullaby.

Or the first time they experience
the presence of the Lord;
as tears flow so freely
you know it's Him they adore.

When they sing their first solo
and your heart swells with pride;
'cause you know it is Jesus
who is living inside.

When they come to your room
with a burden to bare,
and you're able to hold them
and lead them in prayer.

When they write you a poem
that is straight from their heart,
telling you how "special"
you have been from the start.

Then all of the sudden
they've grown up, it appears;
they come with big smiles
and eyes filled with tears;

Mom, it has happened
something wonderful inside;
I believe God has sent him,
I'm going to be his bride.

This is when you realize
that riches aren't gold;
it's moments like these
"They are riches untold."

Safe in the Lighthouse

Oh gracious Father,
God of my soul.
I bring you my heart
for You to hold.
No other place
do I find to be safe
than in your loving arms
and your endless grace.
In your mercy do I hope,
My God, my Lord.
In your mercy do I hope,
forevermore.
For You brought me out
of darkness into light.
You taught me love
and everything that's right.
You have taught me how
to walk each day.
You have brought me back
when I went astray.
Watch over my heart, Lord,
I trust only Thee.
You are like a lighthouse
shining at Sea.

Written March 22, 2005

Seasons of Pain

Another season now passes, Lord
Oh, these seasons of my life
Step by step, hour by hour
I made it through the night

So many tears I had to embrace
As You spoke, "Child, let them flow."
My heart was breaking deep inside
Oh, God, You always know

I ran to You with outstretched arms
I laid before Your throne
The broken heart within me
Was healed as I ran home

Scripture by scripture, prayer by prayer
Loved ones shared that they cared
Arm in arm, hand in hand
Encouraging words were shared

Grace and mercy, peace and hope
Sprang forth like a well
Flowing deep within my heart
Sealing your love as it fell

Sweet victory was mine, Your promise stood true
As praises to You, I sang
I'll rest now in Your arms, my Lord
My gratefulness will always remain!

I praise you, Father,
Your loving daughter, Freda

She Is Not Forgotten

She is not forgotten,
   although her breath has ceased;
She is not forgotten,
   my love has not decreased.

She is not forgotten,
   although I hear no voice;
She is not forgotten,
   for her I only rejoice.

She is not forgotten,
   although I long to feel,
the warmth and love which flowed from her,
   making life wonderful and real.

She is not forgotten,
   she has left so many seeds;
Scattered throughout this world of ours,
   still ministering to other's needs.

She is not forgotten,
   her words I hear so clear;
Trust in God, my Daughter,
   He's always very near.

He'll never leave you
   or go away,
just give Him your heart,
   and walk each day;

Close beside Him,
   'cause His word is true;
He'll never get tired
   of walking with you.

His plan for all
   is to live someday,
in a wonderful world,
   so far away;

Where death nor sorrow
   can enter in,
only peace and joy;
   But not our sin.

She holds a very special place,
   within my heart so deep.
I have so many memories,
   of her I'll always keep.

Although a stone now marks her grave,
   I'm waiting for the day;
With open arms she'll run to me,
   never again to go away …

She Ran the Race

She was sitting amongst the wild lilies …
   The sun was warm on her face …
Looking beyond the horizon—
   Her breathing was slowing her pace …

Her body was frail
   beneath the blue crystal skies,
as she struggled once more—
   To say her final "Good-byes"

She had fought long and hard,
   she had finished her race—
Now leaving her loved ones
   for her Savior's embrace …

The sky—now black,
   had turned into night—
She reached out her hand—
   walked into the light …

Written February 18, 2001

She's Running in Heavenly Meadows

The doctor's words
   rang loud in my ears,
as I struggled for control,
   choking back my tears …

He was holding a part
   of my heart in his hands—
I saw the tenderness,
   in this gentle old man …

My attention now focused
   on the blanket below—
There laid my doggie,
   already turning cold …

Many years of love,
   she had given to me …
Running in meadows,
   and down by the sea …

She never cared what I looked like—
   She never noticed what I wore …
Happiness to her, was playing with toys—
   Just me and her—there on the floor …

I wouldn't trade the pain I'm experiencing—
   It's part of life, as you love …
I know my Father in heaven,
   Is healing me from up above …

Written February 17, 2001

Shine Forth His Light

The Lord is my Lamp
   He turns my darkness into light.
He guides me by day
   and protects me through the night.

He shines His light on my path
   that I might not stumble.
Makes my heart to rejoice
   and my spirit to be humble.

Is my light shining?
   Is it brilliant and bright?
Does it break through the darkness
   and bring forth the light?

Is it revealing to others?
   On my face is it seen?
Reflecting His Glory
   of life within me?

Can my face be read
   by the light it is shining,
giving off the presence
   of God's love abiding?

This is my heart's cry
   to Him who is light.
Make me your vessel
   to shine in the night.

Shine your love in my heart
    and on my face—
Give me open arms
    for the lost to embrace.

Shine Your word
    deep into my soul,
and give me wisdom
    to speak and be bold.

May I never hide
    my lamp under a bushel—
Oh, Dear God,
    never under a bushel …

Someone Is Praying

Someone is praying for me,
   I know that they're down on their knees.
I can see your sweet face, I can feel your embrace,
   because someone is praying for me.

Someone is praying for me,
   I feel the chains of the enemy flee.
My strength's coming back, my focus is clear,
   because someone is praying for me.

Someone is praying for me,
   blue skies on the Horizon I see.
There's a new joy in my heart, a new smile on my face,
   because someone is praying for me.

Someone is praying for me,
   to take the word of your love to the streets;
To be a vessel of hope, your word as my coat,
   they're praying your lighthouse I'll be.

Someone is praying for me,
   they're standing in the gap, Lord, on their knees.
May I be faithful and true, bringing Honor to you,
   because someone is praying for me.

Someone's Hurting

The tears are flowing heavy, Lord,
   my heart is ripping in two.
Someone's crying out, dear Lord,
   they're reaching out to you.

I understand the gift now, Lord,
   you've given me in prayer.
It's not easy at times to carry—
   but the rewards are always there.

As I hide away with you,
   entering your presence in prayer,
you are so faithful to meet the needs—
   of the ones I'm lifting there.

Spiritual Fight

Darkness is all around,
  Oh! How I fear.
Will ever I be relieved,
  of all my tears?

Grasp my hand, Lord,
  please hold it tight—
Guide me through,
  this spiritual fight.

My heart is troubled,
  overwhelming in me—
I cannot see the glory,
  of my Savior Thee.

Confusion reigns,
  in this mortal soul—
Release me, Lord,
  from thoughts untold.

Cleanse my heart
  and set me free,
That I may again—
  Worship only Thee.

Set my eyes
  on things above,
that I might feel—
  Thy precious love.

Make me bold
   so strong and brave,
to help bring souls—
   for You to save.

Cover the dark
   with thy beautiful light—
Together we'll win,
   this Spiritual Fight ...

Spring of Hope

Looking out my window
I see the birds
excitedly welcoming spring;
you can hear it in their voices.

The sun is paving the way
with its warmth
and every day is getting brighter;
the clouds are retreating.

Everything dead now will be
springing forth with new life.
The trees will regain their leaves,
flowers will renew their beauty.

The sun is eager to do its part,
it will bring a warm feeling.
The windows now closed to keep out winter
will fling open to meet the spring breeze.

Wait! I scream, there's something missing!
Spring cannot start,
there's still this coldness
inside my heart.

Tell the birds they must sing louder,
for their sweetness has been drowned;
Ask them to plant their seed of excitement,
within this heart that's down.

Tell the sun I need its warmth
to melt away this icy feeling.
Let its rays go deep to cut
out the numbness.

Tell the flowers, they must grow taller,
I can't see them through the dark;
Ask them to bloom sweeter,
send their fragrance to my heart.

Let the wind send in its gust
to sweep away this heart of crust.
Let it crumble the built-up scabs,
refilling it with its healing salve.

What's that? The smell of a rose?
could it be lifting?
coming forth,
in the "Spring of Hope" ...

Stay on Course

Oh! the freedom
   in the air;
With its beauty
   does none compare.

Clouds so smooth,
   soft and bright;
Reminds me of
   my Savior's light.

Soaring up toward
   heaven's gates,
there is where
   my Jesus waits.

Though my course
   may vary slight,
I will never
   lose the sight;

Of the one
   who walks with me;
I'll keep my eyes
   fixed only on Thee.

I hear His voice
   so sweetly say;
"Stay on course,
   my son today.

Do not waver
  in your faith;
Because my son,
  I'm never late;

With my promises
  to you,
I WILL ALWAYS,
  SEE YOU THROUGH."

Story Time[*]

Now I remember a story
Of an old lady in a shoe
Who had so many kids
She didn't know what to do.

She worried and fretted
The whole day long
She did her best
But she wasn't very strong.

I can hear her now
As she paced through her shoe
"Oh, dear me,
I just don't know what to do!"

My children they have
No food now to eat
I have not a shoe
For to put on their feet.

My cupboards are bare
I have not a dime
I would get a job
But I just don't have time.

Now I have an answer
For this little old gal
I'll tell her of Jesus
And how he's our pal.

* Titled by family

I'll tell her how he
Will meet all her needs
If she'll just get down
And pray on her knees.

I'll tell how he loves her
And went to the cross
To be her dear Savior
If she'll let him be the boss.

Now don't you think
The old lady in the shoe
Would be so much happier
If Jesus she knew?

Do you, my friend
Have loved ones too
That you would like Jesus
To save and renew?

Just believe in your heart
Pray and read
'Cause Jesus has promised
To meet every need.

He cares about you
And your loved ones too
He knows everything
That you say and do.

So if you ever meet
The old lady in the shoe
Walk right up to her
And say, "Jesus loves you!"

Strayed from the Path

Here I am, Lord, with an empty vessel;
   will you fill it up anew?
Precious Holy Spirit, embrace me,
   I need a touch from you.

Dark clouds are hovering above my head,
   I'm fighting to make it through.
A fresh glimpse of Calvary, that's what I need,
   to continue my walk with you.

An emptiness, Lord, in this vessel I feel;
   I've strayed from the pathway to you.
In a moment of time, my eyes have been blind,
   to the hard times you've helped me come through.

Once again, take hold of my hand,
   so gently as you always do.
I'll brush away my pride, put down all my cares,
   and walk down that pathway to you.

Strength Through Adversity

Is your heart breaking in a million pieces,
 you feel you can hardly breathe?
I understand, 'cause I've been there before
 but my God has delivered me.

Is your pillow at night, soaked wet with tears
 from crying uncontrollably?
Don't feel you're alone, you're not, my dear friend,
 God is watching over thee.

Have you looked toward heaven and shaken a fist
 saying, "God, why You picking on me?"
I hate to admit it, I've been there before,
 I was sure He had forsaken and fled.

Have you sat at the bedside of a loved one near death,
 and wondered how you would survive?
Without their sweet smile, their warmth, and their care,
 as they struggled to take their last breath.

Sometimes my spirit deep inside wants to scream,
 as I question my trials before.
But I've walked with my God long enough now to know,
 it's then He won't allow anymore.

I wish I could give you the strength that I've gleaned,
 from the times I've laid broken and torn;
Yet what would it profit if I spared you the chance
 to get it firsthand from the Lord …

Teacher

I listened so intently
to the words she had to say.
She spoke about a loving God,
in a very personal way.

The look upon her face showed wisdom,
she had experienced it; she knew—
The lesson she was teaching—
she said her God would do.

She spoke of *love* "Unconditional"—
He'd give to every child;
She glanced my way, as if to say,
"I mean you" and then she smiled.

Faith arose within my spirit,
a new awareness of "His" love—
Like manna from heaven coming down to me;
I felt new life from above.

Refreshing waves rolled over my soul,
washed clean by this great love—
Like wings of an angel resting on me,
His Spirit like a gentle dove.

Quiet moments in the presence of God,
as my "teacher" uses her "gift."
Anointed by His Spirit, touched by His love,
she's given my soul a new lift …

Tears of War

The War on Earth has ended.
The words ring loudly in my ear.
The weapons now are empty,
smoke-filled streets are clear.

The wounded, the dead, are cared for,
the families notified.
The tears, the grief beginning,
as the planes leave the bomb-filled sky.

Sweet victory, ah, for the moment,
the price so greatly paid.
Now lurking in the shadows,
the foundation has been laid.

The wickedness of man will rise,
for power, for wealth, for control.
The wars not over till the end,
the fight's on for your soul.

It started two thousand years ago,
the angels took their stand.
The good, the bad, the tug of war,
it told the fate of man.

The struggle's been the same throughout;
for power, for wealth, for control.
As Satan and his Demons,
were cast out of the fold.

The fight is dirty, it goes unseen,
the "Spiritual War" is here.
Grab your weapons, "The Word of God,"
and scream it in their ear.

Don't take the slaps upon the face,
the wounds that cut so deep.
Just tell Satan where he belongs,
and the justice he will reap.

Our "Mighty Warrior," our "Prince of Peace,"
has fought and paid the price.
The Victory ours, we've won the fight,
through the "Ultimate Sacrifice" …

Tears Through the Storm

It's okay to ask "Why, Lord?"
    while walking through the storm;
It's okay to seek His face
    from night till early morn.

It's okay to shed a tear,
    it does not make you weak;
It's okay to bare your heart,
    for that's when the Spirit speaks.

It's okay to question
    the Father's mighty plan;
For when you do, He'll speak to you—
    "My child, you're in my hand."

He'll whisper special secrets,
    they'll always pull you through;
Because He has your best at heart,
    you'll know it's just for you.

He'll be so ever gentle
    as He walks through the storm with you;
You can always be content
    because the Father speaks the truth.

He will never ask of you
    more than you can bear;
Even though, at times, you ask,
    "Father, are You really there?"

Sometimes the waters seem so deep,
   you're sure that you will drown;
That's the time to trust Him more,
   He will not let you down.

Just when it seems the darkest
   the light comes filtering through;
It's at that moment in your heart,
   you know He's walked with you.

So it's okay to cry dear,
   don't hide those tears from Him;
Because until they start to flow,
   the healing cannot begin.

He needs the windows of our hearts
   to be flung open wide.
With honest, true sincerity,
   for He knows what is inside.

So now, dear one, please listen,
   for the Father loves you so;
Don't hold back any longer,
   just let those warm tears go ...

Tenfold

You've returned ten times and more,
   great "Blessings" my reward.
You've replaced my love for You—
   Far greater than before.

You've replaced my faithless nights,
   with Worship and with Praise,
You have given songs of love—
   Embraced me with your Grace.

You've put a new shine upon my face,
   how could I ask for more?
Your faithfulness has stood the test—
   "My Savior, Precious Lord" …

Thank You

There's people in our
    world today,
that bless our hearts
    in special ways;

And you are one
    to say the least,
that's blessed this heart
    and brought me peace.

Your wisdom in the
    Lord, my friend,
is far more greater
    than known by men.

Your loving ways
and caring heart;
is truly a gift,
on the Father's part ...

So this THANK YOU
    comes to say;
"God bless you, friend,
    have a great day!"

With His love
Freda Westnedge

Thankful for the Little Things

I'm watching the squirrels You gave me, Lord,
    they're playing in the yard on my tree.
They're hustling and bustling, finding their food,
    as I count now, the number is three.

They trust me, dear Lord, they know they are safe;
    A haven they've found at my place.
As word gets around, new friends I have found,
    the number is eight now at play.

I've taught them to come straight up to my door,
    and take food right out of my hand.
As I watch carefully, their steps very slow,
    I realize I'm part of your plan.

Your creation is fed in one way or another,
    be it man, bird, or beast.
I feel now your love as I reach out to feed,
    these little ones here at my feet.

The Angels Rejoice

Many prayers have been said for you,
    you've been lifted to the Father's throne.
I'm so happy now to hear,
    Heaven will be your new home.

I'm glad you took that step of faith,
    the humble knee you bent.
How the angels did rejoice,
    on the day you decided to repent.

Now the gates will open wide,
    Jesus will come for you;
They'll be my mother and yours there too,
    when your life down here is through.

So if you get there before I do,
    please tell them how much I care.
Tell them that I love them too,
    and I'll meet you all up there.

The Bible

What has my Bible done for me?
   let me try to convey.
It was a very wintry night,
   it came and showed me the way.

I opened up the pages,
   of the gift that I'd received—
began to read the words,
   which my mind would now conceive.

I started at the beginning,
   it told it like it was.
I read about the fall,
   which I was now a part of.

I read of all the sin and shame,
   we brought upon His name.
I read about rebellion
   and all the ugly games.

But as I turned the pages,
   of this strange yet wonderful book—
I read about a sacrifice …
   I needed another look.

I read of a man named Jesus,
   who bled and died for me
and hung upon a cross,
   at a place called Calvary.

My heart began to soften,
   the tears began to flow—
How could this man now die for me,
   of whom I did not know?

My mind began to wonder,
   my lips began to pray—
I know my heart is not the same,
   as it was upon that day.

I had a new beginning,
   from this Bible my mother gave—
I think she really always knew,
   someday I'd find my way.

My Bible's very dear to me,
   without it I'd be lost!
Through it I found my Jesus,
   who paid the ultimate cost …

The Body of Christ

Look around the congregation,
   we all have our place.
Our hearts, we need to open,
   to pray and seek His face.

At the top, we have the pastor,
   we're the flock that he must feed.
He always has a message,
   which meets our every need.

The pianist is important,
   for us to sing the songs.
She gives us her talent,
   the praise to God belongs.

The teachers study in God's word,
   to give their very best.
They know it's not within themselves,
   the Lord must do the rest.

Over there, we have an artist,
   his work is so divine.
He loves the Lord and is sincere,
   he gives to us his time.

We see the ushers as we come,
   into the church to pray.
I know we could relate to them,
   a "Thank you" we could say.

It is so quiet in the church,
    when Pastor stands to preach.
Because there is a saint that loves;
    the babies are her outreach.

Our youth are so important,
    and play a vital part.
They are so bright and spunky,
    they steal away our hearts.

The treasurer keeps the money,
    she has a special way,
and works so hard with love and care,
    but never with delay.

The secretary's work is neat,
    she does so many deeds,
and has to be on time to meet
    the pastor's every need.

We have so many saints who pray,
    for us they intercede.
They ask the Lord to bless and meet,
    our each and every need.

Without the board and deacons,
    we could not run our church.
It's known that they all vote and pray,
    their hearts they must research.

The singers are a blessing,
    they make it so worthwhile.
We hear their voices raise in praise,
    through each and every aisle.

Here we have a poet,
   who writes words from the heart.
I know we can express our love,
   if we will do our part.

The body fits together,
   in such a lovely way;
Will you pray and ask our Lord,
   what you can do today?

The Bond of Friendships

Today, I was thinking
   of how "special" you are.
About all of the times
   you've ministered to my heart.

I thought on the good times
   we've had in the past.
I pray that our friendship,
   will strengthen and last.

My heart was saddened
   as I thought of some pain—
When we had our differences
   that caused our friendship some strain.

But I know that because
   we have the love of the Lord—
We can face these problems,
   and then close the door.

Cause "friendships" are special,
   as God builds the bond—
And "forgiveness" is the foundation
   we're building upon.

Now my day has been blessed
   'cause you came into mind—
I want you to know
   I'm not looking behind.

I'm looking forward
    to what God has in store—
For all who love him,
    and worship the Lord.

For I cherish every moment
of my friendship with you—
And we'll spend together
"Eternity" too …

The Bride

He's coming again, you know, someday;
    Our Lord returning for "His bride."
Are we watching, awaiting, that glorious event,
    or taking it only in stride?

Have we prepared our lamps for Him,
    keeping them oiled, day and night?
Or have cares and pressures of this world,
    caused us to lose hope of that sight?

There's so much talk of love today,
    is it coming from within?
Could it be mere lip service?
    My Lord knows the hearts of men.

So let us on this Valentine's Day,
    which is set aside for love;
Examine our hearts, souls, and minds,
    to be stayed on our Father above.

His bride without spot or wrinkle,
    this our goal should be—
It was the shed blood of Jesus,
    which paid the price you see.

So have you got His covering on?
    for the return is now so near;
Are you waiting for the trumpet to sound—
    "Behold! Our Lord is here!"

There is no earthly love compared,
   to our Lord, our Shepherd, our Guide;
And yes, He's coming—He's coming dear saints,
   for us—His eternal brides!

The Day We Embrace

When the heavens break open
and I see your face …
I'll fall on my knees,
singing "Amazing Grace."

I'll shout with the redeemed,
as we throw you our crowns …
All the angels will sing,
as we gather around …

We'll sing "Majesty,"
for only you, our King …
Are worthy to be honored—
Salvation you bring …

I'll run to your arms,
where safely I'll stay …
Oh Jesus, sweet Jesus,
How I long for that day!

How awesome, my Father,
your love is to me …
Thank You, my Jesus
for setting me free …

Oh Jesus, sweet Jesus,
I long for that day …
When you and I
will finally embrace …

Written April 26, 2004

The Fall

She sits by the window,
   watching the rain.
Her thoughts wander back
   to all of the pain.

How could she have been
   so blinded by sin—
how could she, so easily,
   have given in.

Heart-wrenching thoughts,
   tears flow like a flood.
She remembers her mind,
   how twisted it was.

That which she thought
   to never be her fate,
now was reality—
   unfaithfulness to her mate.

How precious her faith,
   her love for the Lord—
an unguarded moment,
   brought sin to her door.

The "Angel of Light"
   "Satan" he's called,
beckoned before,
   but "never" would she fall.

In a fleeting moment
   the world's thinking seemed right—
a twist of the scriptures—
   her days became night.

Sin was conceived,
   it blinded the light.
Yet for a time—
   she held to it tight.

Oh! but her God
   would not leave her in sin,
as she opened her heart
   to the Spirit within.

Through prayers of the faithful,
   God brought her back home,
with arms opened wide—
   restored to His throne.

One word, let me add,
   please listen as I speak—
Never give up
   on a sister who's weak.

For love covers a multitude,
   of sins we are told—
pray without ceasing,
   with His word be bold.

For the word is sharper
   than a two-edged sword,
piercing the heart—
   breaking through to the core.

It heals and brings comfort,
    to those in distress;
Given in love,
    the Spirit will do to the rest.

So never, please never,
    give up on the weak—
Love them through prayer,
    and our Father will speak ...

The Feast

I see the table,
 the feast is prepared.
An abundance of riches,
 none other to compare.

It all is so lovely,
 its beauty sublime.
It takes now my breath,
 and boggles my mind.

I must make ready
 to enter this feast;
I must put off everything
 when the Master speaks.

"Come now my daughter,
 I'm ready; it's through;
But first go to the highways,
 and bring some with you.

Tell them I love them,
 and I bid them now come.
My feast is for everyone,
 not just for some.

My blood is supplied
 for all to receive;
Now hearken and listen,
 please come unto me.

Tell them I've waited,
  but time is now short;
Enter my children,
  before I must shut the door.

Now take them the message,
  for time is so short;
Please enter my children
  before I must shut the door."

The Gift of a Prayer

You came to mind again today,
   my Father said, "Please pray.
Your sister's under attack my child,
   she's hurting in the worst way.

She's in the battle zone out there,
   she's fighting for souls to be freed.
She has my heart of compassion and love,
   she wants to minister to needs.

Your prayer can be the weapon I send
   to give her strength, new power within;
So please don't hesitate, my child,
   get on your knee, go that extra mile.

For your weapons are not carnal
   they're mighty in me,
And when you pray
   the angels are set free;

To go before her
   tear down walls that are strong—
Guide and protect her
   keeping her safe all day long.

So now you've accomplished,
   what you pray every day—
You've served me, my child,
   in a very special way ..."

The Gift of Easter

I would imagine it was a sunny day
    some two thousand years ago.
There was a stirring about the tomb,
    as the Lord was about to show.

I chuckle to think of the Pharisees
    and the boulder they thought would hold—
Surely it was secure, they thought;
    but God's plan was about to unfold.

A rumbling came as great thunder,
    the soldiers began to fear ...
A light so bright ... it blinded them,
    as an "Angel" did appear.

Mary was first to arrive on the scene,
    she came early on that day ...
To see her "SAVIOR" whom she loved—
    Brokenhearted, she began to pray.

Then in the corner, she saw Him,
    her risen "SAVIOR," she had found.
Strips of cloth lay on the floor
    that once had held Him bound.

Go now my sister to the village
    and tell of what you've seen.
She hurried along with hope in her heart,
    her eyes all sparkling with gleam.

"He is risen, He is risen,"
   she proclaimed as she went on her way.
With joy and excitement within her voice,
   told the Brethren—"He has risen today!"

So try to remember back in time,
   of the circumstances that took place …
And on this Easter Day—Thank our God,
   for His Power and His Grace!

The Goal

The time has come
   and you've worked so hard;
The reward is great,
   God's word is in your heart.

Go now, girls,
   you heard them say;
Climb the staircase
   and win the race.

You set your goal,
   you sacrificed;
gave of your time,
   you paid the price.

The work was hard,
   sometimes you'd fall;
Then God would give you
   one more call;

"Lift up your head
   and hold it high—
Reach for those stars
   up in my sky;

"I'll be your strength
   when in times you're weak,
if you will trust me,
   and my word you seek.

"For I'm your God
    and we'll persevere,
to win that race
    that you hold dear."

So here you stand,
    it's finished now;
You believed your God,
    and you won the crown.

The Last Words

I heard the words
   of a saint today
she told of a place
   so far away.

She told of the beauty
   all around,
she told of the peace,
   that she had found.

She told of a light,
   being glorious and bright;
how Jesus was coming
   for her that night.

She told of the saints,
   she was seeing there;
she said they were coming,
   from everywhere.

Ah, but then,
   she spoke of a friend,
it was her daughter,
   her very own kin.

Someone she'd lost
   so long ago,
someone who died
   before she was old;

And then almost,
   in the very same breath,
she spoke of another,
   that preceded in death;

"Little Philip,
   he's here too,"
that's her grandson,
   he was only two.

Then she spoke
   of the light getting brighter
and as I listened,
   my eyes got wider;

I wanted to see,
   what she saw then,
I wanted to be
   where she had been.

But then I knew
   that I couldn't know,
for where she was,
   I couldn't go.

She spoke of Jesus,
   He was taking her hand,
leading her into
   the promised land;

A heaven prepared,
   for me and you,
we'll all be there,
   when this life is through ...

IN MEMORY OF JOY

The Operation

I have a terrible feeling in my stomach, Lord,
I think it's fear!
Would You please forgive me,
and put your peace in here?

Pastor! I'm so glad you came, please stand over here,
and pray in Jesus's name.
Thank you, Lord, for sending him,
to anoint my head with oil …
I can go to sleep now,
relieved of all my toil.

The Race

I shall run the race, Lord,
with the strength that You give,
and try not to tire,
through the years as I live.
From this day to that,
help me to see,
that onward I'll press,
in service to Thee.
Not looking back,
on the failures I see,
but keeping my eyes,
fixed only on Thee.

The Remembrance Book—
Malachi 3:16

I want to be written in the *Remembrance Book*,
of how I feared your name;
And let it be said since I met you, Lord,
my life's never been the same.

Let it be said that forgiveness of sin,
has been filtered throughout my life—
That You have faithfully loved me, Lord,
whether I did wrong or right.

Yet let it be said and taken to heart,
that we reap what we have sown—
And let it be told, we need to hold,
tightly to the truth we've known.

Let it be said that your power to heal,
has been proven time and again—
You're always there to touch us, Lord,
each woman, child, and man.

Let it be said that it may not be
in the way we understand—
But your Grace is sufficient, your love far surpassed,
we're in the hollow of your hand.

Let it be said that salvation is free,
but it came at a very high price—
Let it be heard that Jesus was sent,
to be our sacrifice.

Let it be said that the pain He endured,
the humility and the blood—
Was not out of weakness; but strength and faith,
and the power of the Father's love.

Let it be said that my serving you
has been a "blessing" and not in vain.
May I bring "Honor and Glory to You
and your Precious Holy Name" …

The Rock

This sure foundation
the rock, our Lord;
This sure foundation,
so lovely and pure.

The winds they come,
the winds they blow;
of this foundation,
I'll never let go.

My sure foundation,
my shield of faith.
I'll trust in you
with every step I take.

My trials they come,
piercing through;
they cannot touch me,
I'm hidden in you.

The fiery darts,
penetrate my soul;
but cannot move me,
as onward we go.

The world lies waiting,
with bondage and snares;
but You brought life,
with freedom to share.

You covered my soul,
with peace and love;
gave me strength and courage,
from heaven above.

You brought the light,
into my dark.
My love for you,
will never depart.

My hope in you,
replaced fear and doubt;
As I clung to your promise,
"We'll work it out."

In childlike faith,
I reached for you;
"Please, Father, help me,
this trial come through."

Just like so many
times before,
You touched my hand,
brought me through the door.

Yes, my trials,
they come and go;
But of God's foundation
I'll keep my hold!

The Search

The world is running
The pace is fast
The cries are silent
Never ending
Help is never heard
Always asked
The search is steady and constant
Where will it end?
The faces have no meaning
Where is the purpose?
What is the reason?
Each to their own
Others matter not
Selfish and self-centered
Dog-eat-dog
Kill or be killed
Stop the merry-go-round
And let me off!

The answer is found
God is waiting
His arms are open
His love gives meaning
His peace slows the pace
The direction is heaven

The Struggle

Why do we fight
So hard against Thee?
Why do we hurt in our hearts?
Our doubt is great
Our souls are troubled
What purpose is our life?
Daily we cry out
"Oh, God, Where are You?"
Our words pound loudly in our ears
We search for ways
To fill the void
All is empty
Nothing satisfies
Life seems so hopeless
Yet the struggle goes on
The fight for purpose
The endless searching for the truth
The deepest thoughts within our minds
Never-ending questions of "Why?"
The heart cries so loud
Where is the help?
God, open the *Heaven* door
Pour wisdom
Answer quickly
Turn not your ears
Open your eyes
Look here at your servant in despair ...

The spirit is contrite and broken
The heart is tender
God has answered

The True Cry

A man must cry to the Lord
From the depths of his heart
Sincerely he cries from within
From his innermost being
He searches with all his heart
For God and His mercy
Then the Lord hears his cry from on high
He rejoices that His lost sheep
Has found his way back
All the angels in heaven rejoice
There is much joy
The lost sheep has come home
He has laid aside the trials of the world
He takes up his cross
To follow once again
The Master and His plan
The burden is light
He wonders what took him
So long to make his decision
He cries over lost time
God wipes his tears and replies
"Hush, child, all is well with your soul
Start fresh, look not behind or in front
Live now, look toward the sky
I come soon to take your hand
Hold fast to my Word, child
Your father is nigh."

The Work Starts Here

As you sit
In church today
Do God a favor
And pray this way

Father, give me
Eyes to see
The lonely hearts
Hiding their hurt from me

Give me ears
To hear their cries
Their silent sobs
With tear filled eyes

Give me a mouth
That speaks words of love
To exhort and encourage
To be gentle as a dove

Give me discernment
That I might see
What's "really" going on
Inside of me

You need my hands
To reach out for you
You need my mouth
To speak words of truth

You need my heart
To be open to Thee
To hear the Spirit
Moving inside of me

So I'll be ready
To answer that call
And go to the hurting
Inside these walls

Those who come each week
All wounded and scarred
From fighting the battles
Which sometimes are hard

Though others are hurting
In lands far and near
Help me to see
My work starts here!

They Sang to Me

I felt the wind
   rustle against my face ...
I heard sweet voices
   singing songs of Praise ...

The room was filled
   with Angelic sounds ...
As they swarmed around me—
   Their words pronounced ...

He's coming! He's coming!
   He's coming, your King!
He's coming! He's coming!
   I heard them sing ...

This Moment and Forever

From the beginning of time
we know not God's plan
His ways are much higher
than the mere thoughts of man.
A long-awaited moment
a dream of the heart
a God-given friendship
to make a new start.
How precious a marriage vow
in the sight of our Lord
His blessing and love
this will be your reward.
As the smell of the rose
is pure and sweet
He'll strengthen your love
from week to week.
Your skies will be blue
yet sometimes they'll gray
but remember "this" moment
God's love is the way!

This World Cannot Hold

This world cannot hold
 a candle to Your love.
Nor give me the peace
 I receive from above ...

This world cannot bring
 me laughter and joy,
the way that You do
 my King and my Lord.

Such beauty and Majesty
 I see in Your eyes ...
This love for You
 will never subside ...

What else can I say
 of Your beauty my King?
I stand here breathless
 as Your praises I sing ...

There once was no hope
 to be found in my heart ...
In You, my Jesus,
 I found a new start ...

You saved me, You redeemed me;
 my Father, my friend.
My love for You is endless,
 it will never ever end ...

Life more abundantly …
   Yes, that's what You gave.
I live only for You,
   now that I'm saved …

I drink of Your water.
   a fountain so free …
It brings out the Joy
   of Your Spirit in me …

Thoughts from the Heart

Thanksgiving always brings to me,
thoughts of loved ones dear.
Thoughts of special friendships,
some far, some near.
Thoughts of precious loved ones,
gone home to be with the Lord.
Thoughts of how they "Blessed" my life,
with love and so much more.
Thoughts of my dear Savior,
and all He's done for me.
Thoughts about the blood,
He shed upon the tree.
Thoughts about how "Blessed" we are,
"A nation under God."
Thoughts about a pending war—
far off on foreign sod.
Thoughts about the young men there,
and women away from home.
I pray for peace and comfort,
for them wherever they roam.
Thoughts of all the tables,
with loved ones all around.
Thoughts of fun and laughter,
and food that will abound.
My heart is filled with "Thanksgiving",
for "Blessings" I hold dear.
Now I pray for you, dear friends—
God's "Blessings" in the coming year.

Written November 28, 2002

Thoughts of the Heart

Oftentimes, people love very deeply …
Yet can't seem to find the words to convey their heart completely …
Please don't ever think that what someone doesn't do or say,
means they don't love you, or think of you every day …
Only God knows the depths of the heart …
Only God knows the words they cannot start …
Only He alone can help you feel
the love in my heart that's very real …

Touch of the Spirit

Hear the wind whistling?
   it's giving a cheer;
The Holy Spirit,
   in our midst is here.

He's hovering over
   each and every one;
Revealing great love
   from the Father and Son.

Oh! how precious
   this third Trinity;
To bestow such an honor,
   on both you and me.

In all His wisdom
   and infinite grace;
The Father has given us,
   a glimpse and a taste.

Through the Spirit
   the mystery's revealed;
A touch to our hearts—
   Now His love is sealed …

Troubled Soul

Trapped inside this soul of mine,
Is bitterness and pain.
I do not want it there, Dear God—
But victory I cannot gain.

I've cried, *Oh Lord*, come set me free—
My words come against the wall.
What will it take to break this bond?
I've said it, You know it all!

I've confessed my sin, my wretched thoughts,
I've cried from deep within.
When will the healing start inside?—
When will it all begin?

The victory is coming, I know it, Lord—
From heaven it's on its way.
The victory is coming, I know it, Lord—
Maybe it'll be today …

True Love

Pen in hand
I want to say
How much I love you
Jesus today
I've pondered deep
From within my heart
Where do I begin?
Where do I start?
You've done so much
For me, my Lord
I am so thankful
I opened the door
You knocked so gently
In my heart one day
Promised to give me
A better way
Of living my life
For I'd made quite a mess
You promised to give me
true happiness
Not from silver
Gold nor fame
But living my life
Through your precious name
A name so pure
Holy and true
You've always done
What you said you'd do
I never knew
what *"true love"* was
till I meet you,
my dear Jesus.

View From the Ferry

Snow-capped mountains
 in the far-distant sky;
Brings God's beauty
 to my wandering eye.

Horizon lined
 with tall fir trees—
Water slapping
 beneath my feet.

Seagulls flying,
 seals at play—
Oh! What a Beautiful
 Glorious Day ...

Blue vast water,
 unlimited view—
Draws my heart,
 Father God to You ...

Wait No More

My goal in life?
Just one—
Point you to the King,
Jesus Christ, God's Precious Son.

He came to earth
as a sacrifice—
Bled and died
to give you life.

He came not as
a King with jewels—
But as a Lamb
to bring renewal.

He waits with open
arms for you—
His love's unending
His heart is true.

This world can't offer
love like this,
nor heaven's gates—
Eternal bliss.

He's reaching out,
He's calling you—
"Come, my child,
it's time you knew.

My love's unending
an open door—
I'm waiting here
just as before.

Take me now
Oh! Please don't wait—
Take me now
Don't hesitate ..."

Walking in the Trials

I've often heard
  my loved ones speak,
of tears they cried,
  on pillows as they sleep.

Oh, how I've hurt
  deep inside my heart,
as the trials they face
  seem to rip them apart.

I listened to a mother,
  who was facing death,
with her precious daughter,
  and the words she said.

I watched her eyes
  and her lovely face,
growing very weary,
  as she fought the race.

And yet I knew
  my God was faithful,
He'd give her strength;
  Help her to remain stable.

As time went on,
  and prayers were prayed,
My God came through;
  Her life was saved.

One more victory
   had been won,
and not by anything
   I had done;

But by our God,
   who honors His word;
It was the prayers,
   that He had heard.

Prayer is the key
   that opens God's heart;
He hears all our words,
   from near or afar.

He's waiting to listen
   as we enter His throne;
Coming with boldness
   'cause we are His own.

He's waiting to answer
   even if it's no;
For He knows what's best
   and where we should go.

Directing our path,
   is His favorite of all;
If we walk in His light,
   we're sure not to fall.

So remember dear sisters,
   as we start a new day;
Our Father is listening,
   if we will just pray.

Warmth of His Presence

Sitting in the shadows of my room,
    soaking in the presence of Your love ...
The quiet, stillness of night,
    brings visions from above.

My thoughts are always toward You, Lord,
    You penetrate my being.
I envision angels before Your throne,
    praising with heavenly singing.

The beauty all around, I see,
    is far greater than words could tell.
I'm captured by the beauty of You,
    as if under a heavenly spell ...

I'm sure there's been a thousand songs,
    poems, and letters too;
That's tried to capture thoughts and words,
    revealing our love for You ...

Your Majesty, my King of kings,
    Jehovah, my solid rock.
I cannot put in human words,
    my deepest heartfelt thoughts.

I'm saturated with love for You,
    my heart feels it will surely burst ...
My precious Jesus, I hope You know,
    in my heart you're always first ...

No other love can touch the heavens,
   nor soar above the clouds.
My heart rejoices in Your love,
   my praises ring out loud.

Listen from Your heavenly throne,
   open your ears unto me—
I give You all my heart, oh Lord,
   as I bow on bended knee ...

Water My Soul

As the rain is food for the flowers,
so is your love, oh God, to me …
It fills the very depths of my soul,
and sets my spirit free …
As the flowers receive their nourishment,
from the fresh new fallen rain—
May I, too, be your vessel, Lord
stretched out to those in pain …
May I be a strong tower,
for them to lean upon—
Bringing hope into their spirit,
to press forward and carry on …
Holy Spirit, breathe your fire,
deep into my soul …
Spread it like a blazing flame—
From my head, down to my toe …
Set my feet to dancing,
give my lips a song of praise—
As I come to You rejoicing,
my hands to heaven raised …

We Can Overcome

I know what you're going through my friend right now,
I've been through the very same things.
I say to You, "Please don't keep it within,
but give it to the King of Kings."
Our problems, struggles, cares, and fears,
the Lord is ready to bear,
if only we'll take the time through our prayers,
to talk with him and share.
To tell him we cannot uphold them ourselves,
but need his ointment of love,
flowing through our lives, hearts, and minds
where the problems we seem to shove.
We all have trails that we must face,
which seem to be such a mess,
but when given to Jesus,
he gives us a wonderful rest.
so out of love I ask you, "Please,
answer that call in your heart,
your cares and all your burdens he'll bear,
and from you he'll never depart."

Wedding Day

I wanted a special gift for you,
yet thought none other would do;
Than opening up my heart and saying,
how happy I am for you.

A Wedding Day, a sacred time;
when you both will say "I do";
And promise to love and cherish each other,
now, and your whole life through.

God blessed the wedding at Cana,
and his face is smiling on you.
His precious grace and perfect love,
will always see you through.

So as you start your life today,
my prayer for you is this;
"Keep Jesus first in your hearts and lives,
and 'His Will' you'll never miss!"

When It's Time

When the call has been made
   and the 'Master' says, "It's time" …
What memories will we leave
   to our loved ones left behind?

Will they remember us …
   for our Laughter, our Charm, or our Grace?
Or possibly just a friendly smile
   upon an aging face …

Will they remember us …
   for words of "Wisdom" that were so great?
Or special notes of "Encouragement"?
   I wonder how we'll rate?

Will they remember us …
   for financial aid we gave?
Helping out when ends would not meet …
   And bills could not be paid?

Will they remember us …
   for our "Luxuries" that we left behind …
Something to make life easy on them,
   in a future realm of time …

What "Legacy" will we leave to them,
   when our time on earth has passed?
This is something everyone,
   at one time in our life should ask …

So when the call has been made,
  and the 'Master' says, "It's time" …
What memories will we leave
  to our loved ones left behind?

When Life Begins

What are you thinking, my little one,
  with eyes so fixed on me?
It sure is a different world,
  than when you were inside, you see.

What are you thinking, my little one?
  About all the noise you hear?
Do you know your mother who loves you so much—
  will always be very near?

What are you thinking, my little one,
  when I hold you close to my breast?
With milk flowing out so warm and free—
  I want to give you my best.

What are you thinking, my little one,
  with blankets around you so warm?
I pray you would feel my heart's desire—
  To keep you from life-long harm.

What are you thinking, my little one,
  of the pain you now endure?
Are you remembering when you were inside,
  feeling safe, protected, and secure?

What are you thinking, my little one,
  when you hear the cry of your voice?
Are you thinking of heaven and no more tears—
  The day we will all rejoice!

So what are you thinking, my little one,
   with that smile upon your face?
I think you're feeling our heavenly Father's
   Love, Mercy, and Grace …

When, Lord?

Lord, I'm so tired
from the trials that I've had,
I'm wounded, and I'm bruised
and sometimes I'm sad.

You've walked with me, Lord
every step of the way,
but sometimes, dear Jesus
I'd just like to say …

"When will all the trials
come to an end?
When is the salvation
for an unsaved friend?

When will there be healing
for the one who has cried?
Where is the victory
for those who have died?

Where is the justice
for the one who brings harm—
to the precious little children
with their cuts and broken arms?

They steal their innocence
like a thief in the night,
and cause them great damage—
it just doesn't seem right!"

My heart gets such pain
when I think on these things,
then the light of your word,
within my spirit it rings!

"I am He who has spoken,
The Omega, the end—
I have not forsaken,
I'll deal with their sin.

I wish none to perish,
I'll write my words in their heart—
If you will just speak it,
then I'll do my part.

I'll bring back those with me,
that I have taken from you—
We'll come with a shout
and the victory too!

I'll wipe all the tears
from the brokenhearted eyes—
They'll be no more pain,
when I descend from the sky!"

If there's one thing I learned, Lord,
through my walking with You—
Your word never changes,
it has always proven true.

So I will just rest now,
put my feelings aside—
Trusting in You, Lord,
and in your *presence* abide ...

When Words Are Not Enough

Can you thank a flower
for its bloom in spring?
Or the golden canary
for the song that it sings?

Can you thank a rose
for its sweet perfume?
or the piano,
for its heavenly tune?

Can you thank a teardrop
for its cleansing flow,
as God brings healing
from sin that we sow?

Can you thank the pain
that brings us closer to Him?
While for the moment
there seems no end.

Sometimes there's feelings
we can't put into words—
yet somehow in prayer,
we know God has heard.

Still I sit pondering
how grateful I am,
for all you've accomplished
for God and His plan.

I marvel at the talents
He's given to you—
How the fruits of the Spirit,
come shining through.

A "Thank You" I know,
is not what you want
But the "Richest of Blessings"—
from the "Anointed One."

So this I can give you
a prayer from my heart—
"I ask you, my Father,
for your "Blessings" to start.

Give *Wisdom* that comes,
from the Spirit alone—
scatter *Your Love,*
throughout their home.

Allow them to see,
through superficial smiles
to minister healing—
to the heart of Your child.

Anoint now their ears
to hear the cry from the heart—
of the "Broken in Spirit,"
whose lives are torn apart.

Crown them with *Peace*
from *Your Heavenly Throne*—
keep them all safe
till You take us all home ..."

When You Think of Me

When you think of me
put a smile on your face
Because I'm hugging you back
in your heart—feel my embrace?

When you think of me
remember the good times we had
Memories last forever—
Someday they won't make you sad.

For now, dear one
please understand,
Your tears are normal
They're God's healing hand.

Where Is My Place, Lord?

Where is my place, Lord?
    Where do I fit?
Where is my chair,
    that I may faithfully sit?

Where is my place, Lord?
what shall I do?
All I want
is to praise and worship you.

What's my call, Lord,
    you've placed on my heart?
What's my call,
    that I may do my part?

Do You want me for
    intercessory?
If so, Lord,
    I will humbly be.

Do You want, perhaps,
    leadership from me?
If so, Lord,
    I need direction from Thee.

Do You want my voice, Lord,
    for praise in song?
or perhaps to make others
    feel they belong.

Do You want me to teach
   the little ones about you?
What is it Father!
   You want me to do?

Where is my place, Lord,
   where do I fit?
Where is my chair
   that I may humbly sit?

Without the Anointing

I know Your strength, Lord.
I know Your power.
I've touched it.
I've felt it.
I've tasted the goodness of my God.

Without Your anointing, Lord
words fall on deaf ears.
Without Your anointing, Lord
words are in vain.
Without the touch of Your Spirit
things remain the same.
It's the *Anointing* that breaks the yoke.

Witnessing on the Highway

It's two o'clock, Lord,
and here again, I'm late,
look at that boy over there,
I wonder how long he'll wait …

What! Out of gas,
how can this be?
"'cause you must go back,
and tell that one of me."

What will I say, Lord,
him I do not know?
"Tell him that I am his friend,
and the right way to him, I'll show."

I'm scared, Lord,
Help me to be strong.
I do not want to say the words,
and have them come out wrong.

He's searching, Lord!
he says he loves You too,
he sure was responsive,
to the words I spoke of You.

He's in your hands, Lord,
I've done all I can do,
I'll just go home now,
and leave the rest to You.

Words[*]

I could write words
That are sweet and sincere
They will make you cry
They will make you cheer
Yet I must use wisdom
To live as I speak
If I say "Don't gossip!"
But then, "Oh, did you hear?"
You will not listen
You'll turn a deaf ear
If I say "Don't lie."
Then, "This one's just white."
Why should you listen
To the words that I write
I know I'm not perfect
And yes, I do sin
But I'm walking in grace
To live what I pen.

*   Titled by family

Worldly Pleasures

I want to lay aside this world,
its thinking and desires.
I want to hide myself in you—
to bask in your presence for hours.

The worldly snares, come swiftly, Lord,
like a storm comes upon the sea;
They get me off the course you've set—
and take my eyes off Thee.

They come in little packages,
all wrapped so pretty and neat.
Disguised with pleasure, marked with sin—
I know it's pain I'll reap.

I need to put my glasses on—
The spiritual ones You give;
That I may see the wickedness
within this world I live.

So I can sail the *sea of life*,
directed by your hand.
Setting my eyes upon the goal—
Your perfect Will and Plan ...

You Are My Hiding Place

When I hide away with you
I am renewed.
When I whisper your name
you hear me and listen.

When I speak to you in prayer, you answer me.
Maybe it's not the answer I'm looking for—
My trust is in *You.*
I have confidence you know best.

When I lift my voice in praise to *You,*
I feel your presence—it over shadows me.
Then my burdens seem light, my worries diminish—
And I am focused on you.

Allowing me to see you more clearly—
To center on wanting only to please you.
Wanting only to walk up rightly with my God.
Wanting only to please *You*—the lover of my soul.

This is my heart's cry to you, my God. May I please only you.
Then will my heart rejoice for your yoke is light.
I can carry it freely—once again, my spirit soars
from just being here hiding away with you.

As the sun rises again tomorrow
I will hide away with you.
You, my God,
the lover of my soul …

Written April 1, 1999

You Love Me Just as I Am

Lord, when You look upon your daughter
Are you proud of what You see?

When you look into my heart, Lord
Do You see my love for Thee?

Do I bring you pleasure
When I bow on bended knee?

Do I make your heart happy
When praises to You, I sing?

Do I make You shed a tear, Lord
When I turn and walk my own way?

Do You feel a little dismayed, my Lord
When I try to carry my burdens, my way?

Lord, I really hardly think so
Since you're acquainted with my grief

Your heart is tender towards me
When I'm sad and when I'm weak

I'm thankful I can be your child
Though many faults have I

You never require perfection
Just only that I try

That's why I love You so, dear Lord
That's why you are my friend

Because you're in my heart tonight
I have victory, I WIN!

Your Love

At times my journey seems so lonely ...
Some valleys get very deep.
I know You are here, Lord, beside me,
though my eyes, at the moment, only weep.

My faith, it sometimes does waver ...
My strength, gets a little bit weak ...
You always are there, Lord, to comfort,
when I bow, in prayer, on my knee.

The enemy may try to surround me ...
He may try to whisper in my ear ...
It's You, Lord, only, I listen to,
It's You, Lord, only, will I hear ...

I'll stand on the firm foundation,
I'll stand with my hand to the plow ...
Remembering your word as my weapon,
I'm rebuking the enemy now!

He must flee, your word has told me ...
When I resist him, he has to go ...
Your Love will cover me completely,
Your Love ... is truth ... to my soul ...

Written February 21, 2000

Writings, Stories, and
Love Letters to God

A Rose, A Heart

The heart is like a flower.
Delicate, beautiful, tender,
yet strong enough to grow in the earth's dirt.

It brings forth beauty in the form of a rose,
when the right soil and pruning has taken place.

It needs to be sheltered from the extreme heat of the sun.
When it's at its full bloom, its fragrance brings a sweet smell of perfume.
If not treated with care, it can wither and die on the bush.
Each rose is different. Called by the Master to bring forth a variety
of color to the eye and fragrance to the senses.

A heart is much the same way.
If it is broken by an unkind word, it can take days, even years for its
    beauty to shine again.
If it is handled carelessly, it can close itself off from the world,
hiding the love and beauty God has placed within.
If not pruned delicately with tenderness, love, acceptance, and
    encouragement, it may stop
beating from mere loneliness.

Let us stop and smell the roses along the way. Let us enjoy their fragrance.
Let us bring forth their perfection; as they have been created for.

Let us treat others carefully and tenderly; as not to break the heart.
Let us extend ourselves to the brokenhearted, the lonely, the rejected.
Let us be instruments of peace; to allow the heart to be everything
    God has created it to be.
Let us not neglect the rose which brings such beauty to the eye.
Let us not neglect the hearts of others that have so much to give; if
    given the right soil …

A Rose in Bloom

When I look into your eyes, I see a delicate little rosebud. I see it gently unfolding into a strong beautiful fragrant rose.

As each petal unfolds, I see some with bruises as they gently open. I see the sun giving them strength. My heart sheds a tear for the pain that was wrapped inside the delicate bruised petals.

As I watch each petal closer, as it gently unfolds before my eyes, I see them growing deeper in color. I smell them as their fragrance becomes sweeter with each unfolding.

Now it's finished. I'm beholding the beauty before me. My heart leaps. Oh, what a glorious sight to behold. Full in bloom for all to see. Standing tall. Reaching for the nourishment of the sun to continue its growth. Becoming more and more fragrant.

I see others being drawn to its beauty. They are enticed by its lovely smell. The aroma fills their heart and gives them joy. Even in the midst of storms it stands firm, unmovable. Reaching to heaven to glorify its Maker. Proud it has come through the rebirth to fulfill its purpose.

God is pleased as He looks down seeing its beauty. Pleased as the sweet fragrance fills Him with delight. I hear Him say, "Well done, my sweet little rose."

June 16, 2004

Eternal Healing

I watched silently as the young man made his way up to the altar. His heart was sincere, you could tell by his tear-filled eyes.

My mind took me back to the countless times before ... when the Spirit moved so lovingly, yet the young man sat cold in his seat. What was different today to change this heart of stone?

Perhaps it started three days ago ... when the young man stood before the tall sandy-haired man in a neatly pressed white jacket. "I'm sorry, sir," the man spoke professionally, "there's nothing I can do for you."

I watched intently as he now knelt before the Father in prayer. The transformation was taking place. The glory of the Lord was shining upon his face. He had received the ultimate touch from "The Great Physician"—healing of heart, soul, and mind.

Oh, why must we wait until the shadow of death beckons at our door, when the Father is forever calling—"Come home, my child," as He stretches out His hands to welcome us into His arms ...

For the Love of My Dad

As far back as I can remember
I have loved you.
Coupled along with fear,
fear of a little child.
I always thought you were the tallest, strongest,
and surely the wisest dad in the world.
Your hands were so strong, and there didn't seem to this little girl
anything you couldn't build with them.
You always seemed to manage catching the largest
And many times more fish than anyone you were with.
I was sure it was because you were so strong
and knew a secret no one else knew.
I remember when times were rough and food was scarce.
I always had trust that you would find some way
of making ends meet and I wouldn't go hungry—
because you were my dad, and you always came through.
When rough times would come to those around you,
even with the little we had,
you were always there to help when they needed a hand.
Your heart was so big.
This was a great example to me—
To do unto others as I would want them to do unto me.
Something my mother always taught me,
since I was a little girl.
I always took every word that you spoke to heart,
and believed in my childish mind you were the smartest dad in
the world. Through the years, your words of truth guided me
and molded my heart to be truthful to myself and those around me.
However, my precious dad, there was a dark cloud that followed
me about during those years, and sadly to say, still lingers until
today. Although words were easily spoken, feelings were put aside.
My feelings, the feelings of a little girl crying out for her love to

be returned.

A little girl trying so desperately to be good enough to win her dad's love. To try to do everything right to make him proud of her. Wondering why the hands that were so strong only seemed to be used to bring pain instead of hugs. Why was I so unlovable, this little heart of mine would question. Why if I reminded you so much of your mother, whom you said you loved, did you seem so disappointed in me. These are questions that would follow me into adulthood and bring many tears throughout the years. As an adult woman in my golden years, I would love to be able to say I have conquered this ghost of my past ... That I have finally achieved enough to make you proud of me, but that's not to be said. The one thing I can finally say is, I still love you, Dad, unconditionally, and I thank you for all you taught me that was good. I have found love that is free, unconditional, no strings attached. Someone who has loved me all my life, even when I was unlovable. Loved me even when I didn't do what he wanted me to. His love has been my strength, and He encourages me when I am sad. He is there for me when all others forsake me. He has never left me, even though I falter. He has proven His love for me over and over. He has shown His trustworthiness to me throughout the years. His love alone is all I need, and I thank you for directing my path that I could meet Him, my very best friend, Jesus ...

Forever Place

I was reflecting on our friendship today, and thanking the Lord for the many times He's met my needs through you. I remember when I was the new "gal" in town; lonely and discouraged. He placed you right in my path, and a friendship began to blossom.

I'll always cherish the weekly prayer time we had together. The many answers to our prayers, and even the ones we are still waiting on. The secrets that we've shared throughout the years are still safely tucked deep inside my heart; only brought to the ears of our heavenly Father.

I remember the greatest gift you've ever given to me; my life as it is today. You dared to risk our friendship by being truthful with me when I almost made the biggest mistake of my life. You gave to me your unconditional love, and without judgment, spoke God's words of life into my spirit. You were truly "God's hands extended" at that time in my life.

Now, once again, you have blessed my life with your sacrifice of love. Your presence at the wedding of my daughter, dear friend, was expressly God's hand to me from above.

I never cease to pray "Blessings" upon you, my friend, and I want you to know ...

You have a *"Forever Place"* in my heart ...

> With all my love,
> Your friend, Freda
> Written May 21, 1996

From the Lord

As I look back over the years, I'm astounded of God's power, the greatness of His patience; the length of His long-suffering.

He wrapped you in a cocoon of protection while He unraveled the tears of your life, allowing you to look in order to be healed, yet secluding you from the damage of the pain. He has kept you close to His heart while teaching you His Word, not letting the tribulations of this world overshadow you. A hedge of protection has been placed around your home; the enemy's darts have been fierce. Fear not, God is with you. He will restore what the cankerworm has eaten away. Hold fast to what He has directed you to do and in the way you are to walk. Know that He is God and does not change. He is firm in His dealings with you for your benefit. Allow Him to continue the molding process. His Love is an everlasting love, and it is not conditional. He knows your weaknesses and will make you strong through them. "Allow me," saith the Lord, "to have full reign in your life, and you will see great and mighty works accomplished."

"I am your God, you are my people," saith the Lord.

"Go forth in the power of my name. I am with you!"

Received Saturday Morning, June 17, 1989

Goldie Finds a Home

One bright spring morning, Bonnie got up very early. She had been so excited the night before; she could hardly sleep. Her father and mother had given her permission to buy a goldfish for a pet.

All night long, the goldfish swam in and out of Bonnie's dreams. Orange ones, big ones, little ones, fat ones, and skinny ones. Now it was morning and time to fulfill her dream!

What will he look like? Bonnie wondered in her mind. *Will I know him when I see him? Maybe "he" will even be a "she."*

It was all Bonnie could do to sit still through breakfast. Food was the last thing on her mind this morning. However, she knew that she needed a good breakfast in order to stay healthy and strong, so she could take care of her goldfish.

After breakfast, she hurried to brush her teeth, running excitedly through the house, she yelled, "I'm ready. I'm ready! May we please go now?"

Mother looked at her and smiled. She understood what a big moment this was for Bonnie. "Yes dear, we can go now! Get in the car, and I'll be right there."

Bonnie ran and got into the car, fastened her seatbelt, and took a deep breath. "Oh, Jesus, I just know You have my goldfish all picked out for me! Please help me to know which one. Thank You, Amen."

The pet store was very busy that day. Bonnie thought to herself, "It must be an important day for these kids too! I hope they find just what they want as well!"

Bonnie's eyes got very big as she walked closer to the fish tanks. There, the fish were all sorts of colors and sizes, just waiting to be picked out and taken home.

She looked in as one small orange fish whipped swiftly by her face. *He was so fast.* She thought he was going to go through the glass! Right behind him, as if they were playing chase, was a larger spotted black one. "Wow," she thought, "It's just like my dream!" Then all of the sudden, there it was, the most beautiful goldfish she had ever seen! It was swimming so elegantly past her as if he were saying, "Hey, look at me! Wouldn't you love to take me home with you? I'd make a great pet! I'll swim around so you can watch me. Why I'd even blow bubbles for you! Please take me home!"

That was it. Bonnie had found the fish of her dreams. He was just what she had envisioned: big, beautiful, and orange!

They picked out the very best fishbowl for him to live in and bought him some tasty food to eat. And yes, it was a "him!"

After paying the clerk her money, Bonnie began to walk toward the car, thinking, "I have just the right name for you, I'll call you GOLDIE!"

They got into the car and started toward home. Looking up to the heavens, Bonnie said another prayer, "Thank You, Jesus. He's just the right one! Amen."

I'm Not There Yet

Dear Lord Jesus,

I'm sitting here in the comfort and safety of my own backyard. The sun is warm on my face. The beauty of your creation is all around me: flowers, trees, birds singing, squirrels gathering nuts for the winter. Life from the outside appears normal. It is amazing how deceiving looks can be.

I purposely used the word "normal" Lord because the world, as we know it, will never be "normal" again. My heart will never be the same.

A burden so great has hit, not only me, Lord, but everyone. Believer and nonbeliever on the face of the earth. Lives have forever been changed. Not in a matter of hours, days, weeks, or years but in a matter of minutes.

The tears, Lord, fall like rain down my cheeks. My heart is forever replaying the dreadful day that our country became the target of such misunderstood hatred. The innocent lives that were taken, the families forever changed by this senseless act of evil; it is sketched in my thoughts forever.

I know I must come to the Cross, Lord, lay this at your feet and leave it there.

"I'm not there yet."

I know I must forgive the monsters who committed this horrible tragedy.

"I'm not there yet."

Your Word tells me to "Pray for these, my enemies."

"I'm not there yet."

My prayers at the moment are only for the innocent, the orphans, the families, and the workers.

"Lord, have mercy, I'm not there yet."

The image of you hanging on the cross between two thieves floods my mind. Your gentle voice speaking with authority beckons my heart to listen to what you said as you hung there innocent.

"Father, forgive them for they know not what they do." It rings again louder. "Father, forgive them for they know not what they do."

"Have mercy, Lord, I'm not there yet."

I have nothing inside of me to give. I pray for Your love. The greatest love. Love that paid the price. Love that sacrificed an innocent life, Your own. Love that covers the sins of the world. Only Your Love can heal my heart. Only Your love can heal our nation.

"Have mercy, Lord, I'm not there yet!"

Written September 22, 2001

In Search of a Friend

Father, here we are again in the calmness of the night. I love moments like this when your presence is so sweet. My "inner being" relaxes after a long day of busyness as I draw strength from you.

I thought of something very special to my heart today, Father. Shall I share with You for a moment or two? I remember as a young child longing to have a special friend. One that I could share my most intimate moments with. I would tell this friend all about my day, all about my victories, and my defeats. I would be able to be myself with this friend and not have to put on a mask, pretending to be something I wasn't. This friend would share my tears and hold me through my fears. I would never have to worry about rejection, for my friend would be beside me every moment. Growth would come from our friendship as we learned more about each other. We would bring the best out in one another as we intertwined to become one.

My search was a long one with many tears and heartaches. I would think I had found this very special friend, when disappointment would come and my heart would be broken. After a while, I would venture out on another search, only to find the same disappointment.

One day, things got very dark, the loneliness was setting in all around me. My dreams of finding this friend seemed so hopeless. Something inside of me was trying to give in to despair when a spark of hope arose and nudged me to try again. "No!" My heart seemed to cry, not again, I don't think I could handle another broken moment. I fought with my heart and said. "Let's try once more, reach out with me to find this 'perfect' friend."

My search lead me far and wide, this time going right up to death's door. There was my friend with open arms reaching to me. I remember the peace I received the moment I met this friend. It was just the way I had always dreamed a true friendship would be. I became very close to this friend, sharing everything with them. No matter what I would tell my friend about myself, I always felt total love and acceptance. My friend promised we would become one, and that I would never be alone again.

By the way, Father, did I share my friend's name with you?

His name is Jesus, your precious son, whom You sent to me. Thank You, Father, He's "PERFECT!"

Your Daughter,
Freda

Lord I'm Waiting

Your creative beauty leaves me breathless—bright, vivid colors splashed on the mountainside. Green, orange, red burst into dance as far as the eye can see.

Clean fresh air brought by morning raindrops. Birds happily flapping their wings as they take their morning baths.

The nip of the air stirs racing thoughts of Fall. How wonderfully You prepared the seasons.

Soon the white-covered blanket of snow will usher in the greatest season. Our celebrations of your greatest gift—Christmas! What a blessed time of year. Jesus will be lifted high; His name on every lip as songs vibrantly fill the sky. Your gift of love in every heart, some not knowing the drive within.

Maybe this will be the year our "waiting" comes to an end.

Come, Lord Jesus!

Love Covers It All

I feel there are many evil pressures coming against our children and families in this day that we now live in. So much so that we could be overcome with great fear if we allowed them to weigh on our minds.

However, as a parent, we must understand that we cannot shelter our families from every bad situation. Our children face, almost daily, pressures from drug addictions, sexual perversion, and immorality.

I believe, as parents, we can protect them from this corruption by being a living example before them, letting the choice then be theirs—showing our love and understanding for others and what they may be going through. By drawing on one another's strength, we can overcome the evils plaguing our nation today.

Let them know, first and foremost, that we are not perfect. We are human, and we make mistakes. Show them that we can learn from our mistakes and better ourselves.

To sum this all up, I've written a poem for "the family."

The Family

God laid the foundation for the family,
this I do believe,
and with the Holy Word he gave,
our fears we can relieve.

He gave us moral standards,
and told us to be kind,
to always put him first,
in our hearts, souls, and minds.

He told us problems would arise,
within our world today,
but not to fear 'cause he had come,
to show a better way.

He walked this earth so long ago,
sowing his seeds of love,
he tried to tell us he had come,
in the name of the Father above.

That we should have no bitterness,
as others sometimes do,
but always a "forgiving heart,"
to say, "Brother, I love you."

Without his love, we cannot walk,
in truth and harmony,
we must extend a loving hand,
to every family.

Reaching out to others, Lord,
let us be the first to say,
"You're always welcome in my home,"
To the Lord, this I pray!

Mary Jane and the Bear Jamboree

Little Mary Jane had a bear that she loved. One day, she thought, "My bear has no friends to hug! It has no Mommy or Daddy or Brothers like I do, no Sisters or family, not one friend or two. I must do something for the bear that I love. He must be very lonely without any friends to hug!"

Mary Jane thought and thought for a while then went running to her mommy with a great big smile. "Oh, Mommy! Oh, Mommy! I know just what to do, please Mommy, please Mommy, will you help me? Will you? A bear jamboree! It will be just the best. We'll invite all my friends to bring their Teddies, all dressed!"

"Lindy could bring Dicky, and Susy could bring Tom. Sherri could bring Theodore, and I know, Arthur would come. He has the triplets. They sing and have drums!"

"I know Charlotte has a bear. It plays the guitar! Oh, Mommy, oh, Mommy, we could make them all stars? Sarah has a bear that plays the piano, and Kailey has one that sings soprano. We'll invite Austin and Megan, and their friend Sue, she has a bear, and he sings too!"

"My friend Julie, she's from the South, you know. She has a big bear. He plays the banjo! He dances and dances and swirls all around. He really has fun! He really goes to town!"

"Debbie, next door, has a bear with a harmonica. It giggles and wiggles. She got it from Monica. Chrissy and Bonnie, the twins on the block. They have a bear that sings in a chair that rocks. And Kim, their friend, has a bear that plays flute! I heard him the other day. Mommy, he's so cute!"

"Do you think, Melissa, the new girl would come? Oh, Mommy, what a great way for her to meet everyone! She has a bear she showed to our class. He's from Germany, and his eyes are made of glass!"

"Remember our postman, Timothy Fellow? His bear is white. It plays the cello! Then, there is

Audrey who lives by the park. She has an angel bear, it plays the harp!"

"I think we have it Mommy! I think we do! I know my bear will love it! Do you, Mommy? Do you?"

Mother replied, "Yes, Mary Jane, I think you do! I know your bear will be happy too!"

So the "Big" day came, with all the bears in one room; they all were dressed up, and some brought balloons! They came in laughing, bears of all sizes and shapes. One bear was so happy he brought a bowlful of grapes!

What a beautiful sight, all the bears with different colors. They all were so happy to be with each other! They danced, and they sang, and they all had a good time! They gave each other "Hugs" as they waited in line!

I looked at my bear, he was laughing and singing. He smiled back at me, and I knew what he was thinking! Then all of a sudden, he was there next to me; He gave me a big hug for the *'Bear Jamboree'*.

My Friend Jack

Jack was a very
   good-looking friend.
He had pretty long hair,
   that blew in the wind.

Such a good friend was he,
   none other had I.
Can you guess who he is,
   from a hint by and by?

He had beautiful eyes,
   that sometimes seemed sad.
If things didn't go his way,
   he often got mad.

He had big sturdy feet,
   that stood firm on the ground,
And everywhere I'd go,
   he'd follow me around.

He had a long curly tail,
   that wagged most of the time.
Except when in trouble,
   he'd drag it behind.

His tongue was so pink,
   long and wet.
Haven't you guessed
   what Jack was yet?

I could tell him my secrets,
   he listened so well.
Never got tired,
   he thought I was swell.

His voice was so deep,
   it rang through the aisles.
Whenever he spoke,
   you could hear him for miles.

He liked to chase cars,
   his favorite sport.
The neighbors said no!
   to the pound they'd report.

My friend Jack,
   you are so neat.
I'll take you to church,
   my Jesus you'll meet.

He'll save you and fill you,
   with such peace and joy.
He'll do it for any
   girl and boy.

What's that you say pastor?
   he's not really a boy?
He can't meet my Jesus,
   or know all the joy?

He's only a dog,
   I'm sure you've guessed now.
But I love my Jack,
   he's a friend anyhow.

Although he's a dog,
    I know Jesus cares,
cause he made all the animals,
        everywhere.

*****

Isn't it wonderful to have a friend like Jack? Someone you can share everything with. All your dreams, all your secrets, even when you're sad. A really good friend like that will always want to listen to you.

I know God is very pleased when we love our animals and take good care of them. He knew the enjoyment we would get from them. That's why they were created.

Isn't it wonderful to know God loved us so much that he even thought about giving us animals to love and care for? I think that's really a good friend, don't you?

Sometimes our animals can't really understand everything we're going through. They can't help us when we need food to eat. If we're sick and need to get well, they really can't help us. Can they?

We do have a friend that can take care of all our needs. Do you know who he is? Shall I give you a few hints?

He came as a babe in a manger. He was born in Bethlehem to a woman named Mary and a man named Joseph. He grew up in a little town called Galilee. His Father was a carpenter. Do you know what a carpenter does? He builds lots of pretty things such as beds to sleep in, cupboard for our dishes, even houses for us to live in. This friend we're talking about grew up strong in spirit and full of wisdom. At the age of twelve, he began teaching the things of God to the religious leaders in Jerusalem. Can you imagine being a teacher at the age of twelve? I think this friend of ours must have been real special, don't you? Let's go on with the story to see if you can guess who our best friend is.

During his growing up years he was very special to God and man. He began performing miracles at about the age of thirty. He did many miracles such as turning water to wine, healing the sick, and raising the dead. Then one day a friend of his turned against him. He turned him into the soldiers who had been looking for him. They didn't like him because he was doing lots of good things for people. They took him to jail. After his trial, he was sentenced to death on the cross.

When they nailed him on the cross, he wasn't angry at them. He began praying for all the people that were doing bad things to him. They thought, if they killed him, he wouldn't be able to do good things anymore. But do you know what happened? He rose from the dead, and he is still doing good things for people today.

Have you guessed who our best friend is yet? That's right! His name is Jesus. He died on the cross so we could be saved from all our sin. What better friend could we have than a friend who would give up His life for us.

I know if I were in any danger, my friend Jack would come to my rescue also. He would protect me from any harm just like Jesus would.

However, Jack is only my dog and cannot meet my needs like my best friend Jesus.

Do you know Jesus? Is he living in your heart today? Why not bow your head right now and ask Jesus to be your best friend. Do you know what will happen then?

YOU'LL HAVE THE BEST FRIEND IN THE WHOLE WIDE WORLD!

My Heart Cries

There's not a day that goes by that my thoughts are not turned heavenward toward my God, my Savior, Jesus Christ, my Guide, my Comforter.

I cry out daily for God's mercy, for His forgiveness of my sins, for His healing power and

long-suffering to envelop me, for His unconditional love to flow through me, for His wisdom to penetrate the very depth of me—giving me true understanding of who He really is!

I'm ever crying out to know Him intimately, to feel His presence so strong as if to feel warm air blowing up against my cheek, to feel His arms so tightly engulfing me so that I would know I was totally and securely safe from all harm.

I cry daily for His Will, not mine; for His direction which will lead me into all truth; for His revelation of light into the world which is the lamp unto my feet; for His Spirit to quicken my mortal body and empower me to go forward in service unto Him.

Never for a moment do I want to think that I have everything He wants for me. I will forever search for the one thing I was created for, the one thing that He longs for me to find—HIS EVERLASTING LOVE!

That's what I was created for—TO LOVE HIM!

My Life I Give*

Father, I love You. I don't think there's any one thing or person that I think of more than You. You're forever on my mind, always in my heart. My thoughts are never far from Thee. I see your beauty all around me. I feel your love even in the lowest times of my life. Those times when I feel overwhelmed, You are still there strengthening my spirit, lifting my eyes heavenward, teaching me the important things in life, teaching me to love the way that You love. To forgive as I've been forgiven. To share as I have been blessed. To open my arms to embrace the lonely. To open my ears to hear your voice. To ready my feet to go where You direct. To take the promises in your Word and share them with others. To live life daily—Yet always waiting for your return. To have a burden for the lost, for the sheep that have gone astray. I know of no greater joy in life than to have You as my friend, my Father, my Redeemer.

This writing was a love letter to God written around the edges of a "property listing" paper as Mom and Dad searched for a new home in Vancouver, Washington.

That's how Freda (Mom) wrote—wherever she was, whatever she was doing, she would stop and pen down the words God gave her as well as her love letters to Him!

---

* Titled by family

My Love, My Devotion, My Heart

Today, we'll start our lives together
Built on trust as our love has grown
I knew from the moment I spoke to you
You were the one I wanted to share my life with
Our hearts connected immediately
As God directed our paths to each other
It was destined from the beginning
I'm glad you waited for me to find you
We have so much in common, you and I
Sharing many of the same interests
However, I want to give you space
To continue to grow into the person
God has made you to be
I know you, too, want the same for me
As we build our lives together, my friend
Our love will grow richer as we keep Him
At the center of our love for each other
Love is not just a fuzzy feeling
I get when our eyes meet across the room
Or a feeling from a warm embrace from you
It's not just from a passionate kiss we share together
True love is devotion to one another
It's me putting your needs ahead of mine
Being committed to each other
Even during the stressful times
That will inevitably come our way
Real love stays strong though the storms of life
Grows deeper with each painful growing period
At the end, it makes one complete circle
A circle of family ties

That started with my love for you
Till death do us part, my friend
This is my commitment to you and to "Our God"
May He "*Bless our Union*" here today!

Spreading Your Wings

The room is empty now. There are marks on the walls where once your pictures hung.

I can no longer feel your presence as I walk into the room where just a few short days ago, you laid sleeping.

I miss walking into your room to greet you with the new morning. I miss our chitchats about the plans for the day.

You're on your own now where you belong. You must make your mark in the world as I have done. Detachment is never easy yet a necessity of life.

I remember the first day I brought you home from the hospital, my beautiful bundle of joy. You were my sunshine in the morning, even on cloudy days. Every day was a new experience, growing together and bonding in friendship.

I remember you at the early age of five, looking so sad and helpless when you had to go through major surgery. I watched your eyes light up as a four-feet stuffed giraffe came bouncing into your hospital room. It seemed to be just what was needed at that moment to speed up the recovery.

Just a short while after while riding down the road singing songs to Jesus, I watched the tears stream down your little cheeks, hands raised to heaven as you felt the presence of God fill the car. I dried those same tears during the years of heartache and pain as you grew into adulthood.

Now the time has come for you to leave the nest. I find myself wanting to wrap my "wings of love" around you again to keep you safe. Yet I know as I release you into the arms of your heavenly Father, His wings will be wrapped securely around you. You will be safe in His shelter.

So I say goodbye, my precious baby daughter. Grow in God's grace.

I love you dearly,
Mom

Tell Me

Tell me about the love You have for me. Whisper
it to me as I'm down here on my knees.
Tell me how You love me, Lord, no matter how unworthy I feel.
Tell me how it's only because of You that I live, feel, cry, and sing.
Tell me how You will always walk with me through
storms, through blue skies, through pain,
through happiness.
Tell me how I make You smile as we sit and fellowship for a while.
Tell me how You knew my name before I knew yours.
Tell me how You searched for me, until I FOUND YOU.
Tell me how You know the bad in me but see only the good.
Tell me how You can love me so much knowing the sin
I would do. Tell me, Lord, I need to hear from You!

Written May 13, 2004

The Long Search

A feeling of wanting to scream is welling up inside me again.
I hate myself as I fight not to give into my weaknesses.
My eyes just want to slumber to get away from the battle.
I walk around in a daze, wondering what to do next to keep my mind
    from whispering to me.
The gray clouds keep smothering me and hiding His face.
I fall on my knees to try to get release for a while.
I feel safe momentarily.
If only I could stay here forever.
What is reality right now?
What is important, and who am I?
How did I lose myself, and where do I find me again?
Oh God, stop the tears before we have another flood on our hands.
    What are we walking through now, Lord?
Is there even an ending to the searching?
Will there also be a healing for me this time?
Oh God, I pray, YES!
Maybe this healing will be the one that makes me whole, makes
    me the person You intended me to be right from the very start
    before all the garbage was dumped in.
I remember for a moment, the darkness I've already come through.
Oh, Father, must I go through the dark again? It was so painful.
Yet I remember our most intimate times together as You held me so
    tight in your presence.
Will You promise to walk with me once more?
I know then that everything will be alright.
As You reveal me to myself, help me love me just the way I am.
Don't let me try to hide from You the way I hide from others.

Know the depth of me, and help me to face myself that I might come to know "me!"

Father, I do want to know "me," and I want to be a "me" that is pleasing to You.

I want only to serve You, and to love You.

That's the dream that I have for myself!

The Thief of Busyness

I sat pondering one day, talking things over with the Lord. I said, "Lord, I know from my previous experiences there's always something I can learn through what You allow to come into my life. However, I've really been trying to sort this one through in my mind. I must confess, I'm not getting a clear picture this time."

You see, the pain in my shoulder had been growing intensely harder to endure. As I recall, it all started over eight months ago with long intervals between. Nothing really too painful that I couldn't busy myself with "important" things like trips to the coast, trips up North to visit my family, trips to Utah to visit my children and grandchildren. All my little craft projects, now they must get finished, Lord. Remember, Christmas is just around the corner.

However, it didn't stop there, did it, Lord? Christmas came and went. I continued my busyness, throwing myself even deeper into my craft projects—because now summer was coming, and things are needed to be done for all of the summer bazaars.

Now I must admit that it took a few moments for the light bulb to come on in my mind. I was spending less and less time with You, Lord, and You were missing my fellowship. You knew that too much of a "good thing" could be bad. I was forgetting how to be still and quiet before You, allowing my busyness to rob me of special times with You—times when your presence would fill me with such awesome awareness of Your Glory, Power, and Love. I was quickly losing my ability to listen to that small still voice that beckoned me.

The pain multiplied to the point that I could not even focus on one individual thing. I centered my thoughts on the pain, not the root cause of the pain. It wasn't until I began to look at what I was reaping through my pain, that I began to understand, that this, too, was working for my good. I was being forced to not busy myself. I was literally being forced to sit when I would rather be on the move. I was denied sleep due to the intense pain which spurred me to turn my thoughts to You continually. I was unable to do housework of any degree which gave me time to sit and meditate on Your Word and to pray more with each passing day.

I sit here now at the latter end of this affliction, reminiscing of how once again You have proved faithful to me!

You touched me when I no longer could endure the pain.

You gave me peace as my mind became stayed on You.

You restored our intimate times together.

You taught me once again how to be still before You.

Even though the pain has greatly subsided, and I could busy myself somewhat, I find again; I desire to sit at your feet to feel your presence and learn what it is today, Lord, that You have to teach me.

Thank You, Father, for this experience through pain.

Touching God's Heart

As I was thinking of you today, warm memories
flooded into my heart.
I remembered the many hours of prayers we have
shared together for our friends and family.
Wet tears running down our faces as we placed them
before the throne room of God.
Seeking His mercy, grace, forgiveness, and
Salvation for each and every one as they came to mind.
I know the scriptures tell us God puts our tears in a bottle.
He records them in His book, someday He will wipe them all away.
His command is to pray without ceasing.
My remembrance of our times together brought a
rekindled love in my heart for you.
The prayers remembered, bringing refreshed hope to
my spirit.
Looking forward to the time we can once again share
our hearts before the throne room of our God.

Watch and Pray

Song:

Help me watch and pray, Lord,
   help me watch and pray.
When the hour is late, and You bid me awake!
   help me watch and pray.

Place a burden on my heart,
   Lord, I do want to pray.
Place a burden on my heart,
   help me watch and pray.

I don't want the easy life,
   Lord, help me watch and pray.
Keep my eyes stayed open wide,
   help me watch and pray.

The time is ticking by so fast,
   help me watch and pray.
The field to harvest, white at last!
   help me watch and pray.

My eyes do slumber, I pray they'll not.
   Lord, help me watch and pray.
The field to harvest, white at last!
   Lord, help me watch and pray.

The field to harvest, white at last!
   Lord, help me watch and pray.

What Is a Mother?

A mother is someone who is always there when you need her.

She is loved and respected by everyone.

She has learned much wisdom through life's experiences and passes it on to her children by example.

A mother is someone who cares deeply for her family, would never go to bed without checking the doors first and sleeps with one eye open.

She has kissed many a scratched knee when the sidewalk happens to jump up and bite her little toddler.

A mother is someone who can frown and say "I love you" at the same time.

She always sees the best in her children and has a God-given desire to meet her family's every need.

A mother is someone who goes to the store to buy herself a new dress but somehow winds up with one for her daughter instead.

A mother is one who prays for her children daily.

She always desires God's best for them and not what she thinks is best.

She is someone who is used to losing many hours of sleep when her children are sick.

She is always there when you need her!

A mother is someone who thinks she cannot darn one more sock or patch one more pair of pants.

She is someone who has a special talent for giving her love away to every member of her family and makes sacrifices for their good.

A mother cooks delicious meals yet sometimes throws in frozen dinners when there just isn't enough hours in the day to get everything done.

A mother is someone who says she's going to bed early tonight!

She's someone who has one more sheet to change before she can read her book.

She's always there when you need her!

A mother is someone who takes your turn at the dishes when you just can't seem to get your homework finished.

She waits with an open ear for the sound of the door opening signifying her last child is home safely.

She has an unending flow of love for her children whether she has one or ten.

She's someone who waits for a good night kiss and a hello smile in the morning.

A mother's work is never done!

She's someone who fixes her child's broken toys.

She's always there when you need her!

A mother is someone who feels the pain of her infant's first shot and fights back the tears when she sends that same child off to kindergarten.

She's someone who fixes you hot soup when you're sick.

A mother is someone who never seems to run out of a kind word even when you don't want to hear it.

A mother is someone who beams when her little girl says, "Mommy, I want to be just like you when I grow up."

A mother is always there when you need her. SHE IS LOVE!

She has learned through the years to lay her children at the feet of Jesus for Him to mold them into His good pleasure and not hers.

And like the Bible promises us in Proverbs 31:28, "Her children arise up and call her blessed."

Wisdom to Change

You know the hidden treasures of my heart.
You know the hidden thoughts within my mind.

You know the hidden desires within me.

These are what I want You to rip out of me, Lord.
I raise them to You now, covered by the precious blood of Your Son.
Cover me with His righteousness and set my spirit free. I want to worship only You.

These things will pass in the blinking of an eye.
My eternal home with You is my true and only desire.
Replace in me, Father, a heart pure and simple with only You at the center.

Restore unto me the joy of my salvation. Put back on my face the smile that only Your presence can bring. Restore the laughter that comes from knowing Your love and peace. Bend my knee once again to the heart crying for prayer.

Bring back the joy of tears shed for the lost. Bring back the hunger and thirst for Your precious Word, that daily I would eat the only food that truly satisfies me. Bring back the Wisdom that leads my feet in the path You have directed me to walk.

The Wisdom that gives me security and comfort.
The Wisdom to choose the right from wrong.
The Wisdom that allows me to know You deeper.

This Wisdom that compels my heart to set my house in order.
This Wisdom that brings me here to my knees, revealing to me to look up, for my redemption draweth nigh …

Written March 30, 1999

Wounded Soul

She walks around in a daze, trying to grab onto a strand
of sanity. Her mind barely able to retrieve a thought.
How long now had the streets been her home?

Tears are a thing of the past, replaced now with walls of
protection, placed there to keep out the pain of rejection.

Oh, how thoughtless is humanity. How insensitive we've
become. Untouchable to the outcast and downtrodden.
Their anger is lashing out at us while inwardly pleading to
be loved and accepted. Accepted for who they are, not what
we want them to be. We pour them into a mold. If, perhaps,
they don't fit, we dump them out and start over. Trying
desperately to shape them into our image of acceptance.

What are we really trying to do? Possibly we're trying to mold
ourselves. Maybe we're seeing in them what we don't like about
ourselves, and we are trying to change at their expense.

There is a great cost involved in dying to one's self and putting
on the image of Christ—to be able to see through His eyes, feel
through His heart, accept through His unconditional love.

To be true followers of Him takes a strength that lies not within
our human resource. It is far beyond our capacity to love. He will
grant us this great gift of His, but first we must count the cost.

Are we ready to bear the marks of Christ? To suffer as He
suffered? Die to self as did He? Are we ready to lay down
our lives for the brethren? There are "wounded souls"
out there walking in despair. God's heart is pleading,
"Please feed My sheep. Please feed My sheep!"

Dedication Poem

This poem was written by Freda's daughters shortly after she passed away.

To the best mother we could ever be blessed with. WE MISS YOU SO MUCH!

Another Day

Another day has come and gone,
I barely made it through,
my day was spent in a hazy fog,
remembering times I'd spent with you.

The memories come and go so fast,
how I wish I could make them stay,
visions of your smiling face,
telling me "Everything'll be okay!"

It's so hard to keep my focus here,
I'm always thinking of heaven above,
imagining you on those golden streets,
rejoicing and having fun!

You were my rock on shaky ground,
the one I was always running to,
the earth now seems a lonelier place,
my heart longs to be there with you.

I know my time will someday come,
I still have work to do,
I'll try to walk each day in love,
just like you taught me to.

I'll say a prayer each day I wake,
"Please help me make it through,
Jesus be my joy and strength,
till I see those gates and you."

Love,

Your daughters